PRESS GANEY®
THE PRESS GANEY SERIES

Making it Right:

Healthcare Service Recovery Tools, Techniques, and Best Practices

Paul Alexander Clark, MPA
Mary P. Malone, MS, JD

HCPro

Making It Right: Healthcare service recovery tools, techniques, and best practices is published by HCPro.

 5 4 3 2 1

ISBN 1-57839-724-3

HCPro, Inc., provides information resources for the healthcare industry. Advice given is general. Readers should consult professional counsel for specific legal, ethical, or clinical questions.

HCPro, Inc, is not affiliated in any way with the Joint Commission on Accreditation of Healthcare Organizations, which owns the JCAHO trademark

Paul Alexander Clark, MPA, Co-editor
Mary P. Malone, MS, JD, Co-editor
Shanna L. Halpern, Senior Managing Editor
Mike Michaud, Bookbuilder
Pat Campagnone, Cover designer
Erin Callahan, Executive Editor
Kathryn Levesque, Group Publisher
Jean St. Pierre, Director of Operations

Arrangements can be made for quantity discounts. For more information, contact:

HCPro, Inc.
P.O. Box 1168
Marblehead, MA 01945
Telephone: 800/650-6787 or 781/639-1872
Fax: 781/639-2982
E-mail: *customerservice@hcpro.com*

Visit Press Ganey at its World Wide Web site: *www.pressganey.com*
Visit HCPro at its World Wide Web site: *www.hcpro.com*

11/2005
20641

Contents

About Press Ganey

This book is based on Press Ganey's research and experience. Founded in 1985 by renowned medical anthropologist Dr. Irwin Press and accomplished social research methodologist Dr. Rodney Ganey, Press Ganey has conducted research in the healthcare field that has provided a novel scientific foundation for assessing patient satisfaction with the experience of care. Over the past 20 years, Press Ganey researchers have honed this system through continuous original qualitative and psychometric investigations to arrive at an unrivaled system for measuring, benchmarking, and improving the satisfaction of patients, employees, and physicians—healthcare organizations' key customers. Today, Press Ganey has dozens of researchers and hundreds of consultants who collaborate not only to help our clients improve but also to ascertain best practices among our top improvers and high performers.

As part of Press Ganey's ongoing best practices research, we conducted two separate studies involving our partners. The first is a statistical analysis to determine which healthcare facilities were "most improved" based on the measure "Staff response to your concerns and complaints"—a standard question on most Press Ganey surveys. We conducted methodologically sound qualitative interviews to ascertain the best practices they deployed to achieve their improvements. We then performed a systematic literature review to determine what best practices already existed related to this issue. Service recovery emerged as one of the strongest best practices for improving patient satisfaction.

Second, we held a contest among all of our 6,000 healthcare facilities to find the best service recovery program. We received dozens of detailed entries, which a team of consultants thoroughly evaluated and rated. The best-rated service recovery programs were honored with public recognition and awards.

These world-class programs and their tools, techniques, and best practices featured in this book come from the following Press Ganey clients who have successful implemented service recovery programs:

- Advocate Healthcare
- Baptist Outpatient Services
- Beebe Medical Center
- Bothwell Regional Health Center

- CaroMont Health
- Carondelet Health Service
- Centra Health
- Columbus Regional Hospital
- Emory Healthcare
- Floyd Medical Center
- Froedtert Memorial Lutheran Hospital & Medical College
- Genesis Health System
- Gottlieb Health Resources Hospital
- Havasu Regional Medical Center
- Henry Ford Wyandotte Hospital
- Holzer Medical Center
- Jefferson Regional Medical Center
- Lexington Medical Center
- Memorial Hospital at Gulfport
- Regional Medical Center/Troyer Clinic, Russell Medical Center
- Saint Luke's Hospital & Health Network
- Saint Vincent's Hospital
- Scott & White Hospital
- SHARP Metropolitan Medical Campus
- Southern Ohio Medical Center
- University of Michigan Hospitals and Health Centers
- Waukesha Memorial Hospital
- Western Maryland Health System
- Women & Infant's Hospital of Rhode Island

This book comes with a CD that includes sample brochures, training programs, service recovery toolkits, and other contributions from Press Ganey partners. It also has a DVD with video clips that illustrate common service recovery situations. Note, however, that these clips don't demonstrate "perfection." There are multiple good ways of handling different situations, and your staff can easily identify different, more effective, or less effective ways of handling these scenarios.

About the Editors

Paul Alexander Clark

Paul Alexander Clark, MPA, is senior knowledge manager for Press Ganey. He directs a team of researchers who conduct quantitative and qualitative research to determine best practices for improving patient, employee, and physician satisfaction in healthcare. His team's research supports more than one hundred Press Ganey consultants who actively partner with healthcare organizations to help them improve the service they provide to patients, employees, and physicians.

Clark has published articles in such journals as the *Joint Commission Journal on Quality and Safety*, the *Journal for Healthcare Quality*, the *Journal of Nursing Care Quality*, and the *International Journal of Healthcare Quality Assurance.* His research has been presented at the annual conferences of the International Society for Quality in Health Care, International Society for Research in Healthcare Financial Management and the Medical Group Management Association as well as the Press Ganey National Client Conference and Johns Hopkins University Institute for Spirituality & Medicine.

Clark earned his Master of Public Administration in science and technology policy from George Mason University in Fairfax, Virginia, and his bachelor's degree from the University of Pittsburgh. He will soon complete a Master of Arts in Bioethics and Healthcare Policy at the Loyola University in Chicago.

Mary P. Malone

Mary P. Malone, MS, JD, is president of Malone Advisory Services in South Bend, IN. She has over 20 years of experience in the healthcare industry. Prior to forming her own firm, she worked for Press Ganey Associates for more than 14 years, serving in a variety of senior leadership positions.

Malone writes and speaks often on various aspects of patient satisfaction. Her articles have appeared in such journals as *Joint Commission Journal on Quality and Safety, Strategies for Healthcare Excellence, Healthcare Financial Management* and *The Satisfaction Monitor*, a client publication of Press Ganey. She has spoken at many national conferences and workshops including the American College of Healthcare Executives, Forum for Healthcare Strategists, Society for Healthcare Consumer Advocacy, the Institute for Healthcare Improvement and various state hospital associations.

Malone earned her law degree from University of Notre Dame Law School and her Masters in Health Administration from Rush University Medical School.

CHAPTER AUTHORS

Randy Blum, Staff Consultant for Press Ganey, is skilled in continuous education for customer service excellence and on-site training. His background is in operations management and computer training. He graduated from the University of Notre Dame with a bachelor's degree in Finance.

Matt Davis, Lead Consultant for Press Ganey, is skilled in continuous education for customer service excellence and public speaking. He has worked in an Inpatient Rehabilitation Unit and Emergency Department. He graduated from Indiana University with a bachelor's degree in Biology.

Tracey Doubrava, EdM, Lead Consultant for Press Ganey, is skilled in defining goals and action plans for service excellence efforts. Her background is in nonprofit and for-profit management and consulting as well as extensive experience in public speaking and personnel training and development. Tracey earned an EdM in Counseling Psychology from Columbia University Teachers College and a BS in Psychology from Union College.

Katie Drevs, Primary Consultant for Press Ganey, is skilled in data collection and interpretation integral to developing and implementing successful satisfaction measurement and improvement programs across large healthcare systems. She received her education from St. Mary's College and the University of Phoenix in Behavioral Health Sciences.

Peggy Fuerbringer, Staff Consultant for Press Ganey, is skilled in proactive problem solving and passion about service quality. Peggy earned a bachelor's degree in Law and Society from Purdue University.

Michelle M. Gloss, MS, Staff Consultant for Press Ganey, is skilled in data interpretation and statistics, and root cause analysis. Her background is in healthcare research and administration. Michelle earned an MS in Healthcare Management from the University of New Orleans and a BA in Sociology from Indiana University.

Scott Holmlund, Regional Service Manager for Press Ganey, is responsible for all day-to-day operations of consultants delivering service to the West Coast. His background is customer service management. Scott graduated from Bethel College with a Liberal Arts degree.

Richard Jun, Staff Consultant for Press Ganey, is skilled in customer service for patient satisfaction. He has an extensive background in employee communications. He earned his bachelor's degree from Purdue University.

Kelly Nemeth, Staff Consultant for Press Ganey, is skilled in helping large systems measure and improve patient, employee and physician satisfaction. She earned a bachelor of science in Consumer Sciences and Retailing from Purdue University.

Aris Relias-Clark, Senior Consultant for Press Ganey Employee Perspectives, is skilled in the project management and leadership for developing effective, practical approaches for employee satisfaction improvement initiatives. Aris received her bachelor's degree from Indiana University.

Deborah Spite, Lead Consultant for Press Ganey, is skilled in non-hospital-based quality improvement. She recently authored the *Promoting Performance Improvement* guide to internal communications on health care quality and, in her personal time, a modern novel titled *The Trouble with Staying* under the pen name Deborah Flora. She earned a bachelor's degree in English and French from Indiana University.

Julie Tittle-Plank, Senior Consultant for Press Ganey Employee Perspectives, delivers enthusiasm, knowledge, and experience to their employee-focused quality improvement initiatives. She earned a bachelor's degree in Spanish and business from Northern Michigan University

Barbara Van Holsbeke, Staff Consultant for Press Ganey, applies her experience in health care to help her clients improve patient satisfaction. Her background is in the legal and healthcare publishing industry. She graduated from Indiana University with a BA in English.

Dedication

This book is dedicated to all of our partners in all of our client healthcare organizations. The work you do as healthcare professionals inspires us every day. We're honored to serve you. Thank you.

This book is especially dedicated to the healthcare professionals who stood at their posts through the Hurricane Katrina disaster and long recovery. You sacrificed personal need to give in service of others and made everyone proud. We can't say it any better than our President and CEO, Mel Hall, "The daily miracles that continue to be performed by those in the healthcare profession leave me speechless and thankful. We stand in awe of you. We give thanks for you. We hold all of you in our thoughts and prayers."

FOREWORD

This book touches the heart of healthcare. Service recovery is the ultimate failsafe that can guarantee an outstanding service experience. Service recovery empowers great people to do great things for patients and residents. Empowered with service recovery, care providers can radically transform negative emotions to positive emotions—from fear to calm, anger to contentment, disappointment to pleasant surprise, and negative outcomes to delighted customers. Employees who create and witness these transformations are excited and satisfied by the special, even magical, moments that make patients' lives a little better. Perhaps no greater employee motivator exists than when people who feel the calling to help people see their purpose fulfilled.

Press Ganey consultants visit hundreds of healthcare facilities every year. Through their intense interaction with our customers, the consultants are witness to, and help create, great service. I have the privilege of working with nearly 480 associates at Press Ganey who bring a missionary zeal to their work of helping our customers improve their delivery of care. This book is a representative sample of their expertise and enthusiasm.

We are honored to partner with more than 6,000 healthcare facilities and provide them with information and solutions that help them serve their patients, physicians, and employees. We walk with them on their ongoing journey to continuously improve, and toward our mutual goal of improving the delivery of healthcare.

Melvin F. Hall, Ph.D.
President & CEO
Press Ganey Associates, Inc.

PART I

INTRODUCTION

Chapter 1

The healthcare landscape

Paul Alexander Clark, Matt Davis, Katie Drevs,
Peggy Fuerbringer, Michelle Gloss, Deborah Spite

The healthcare marketplace is changing to emphasize, recognize, and include service quality as part of the total quality picture. Clinical quality refers to the quality of patient care and treatment provided by the physicians, nurses, licensed independent practitioners, and other clinicians—and is often assessed by looking at information about structure, process, and outcome. That is, it examines what actually happens to the patient.

Service quality involves everything that relates to providing that patient care. The bottom line is still, in essence, what happens to the patient, but this time we are looking at information such as how long a patient must wait on a gurney for an x-ray, how friendly the meal service provider is, or how clean the halls are. To patients, the most important aspects of service quality involve fundamental issues of communication, respect for personhood, involvement in decision-making, emotional needs, and psychosocial care.

Paying for quality

Policy experts widely expect that incentives for technical and patient-perceived quality will soon flow from all major payers, including the Centers for Medicare & Medicaid Services (CMS). In the 2006 fiscal year, hospitals participating in the CMS Voluntary Quality Initiative quality data reporting program will receive a payment increase of 3.7%; those not participating will only receive 3.3%. It is only a matter of time before these incentives turn into bonuses for improvement (as has been shown in several pilot programs). It is also only a matter of time before this policy starts to be applied to non-acute healthcare services.

Finally, the Hospital Quality Initiative (HQI) has a patient perspectives component known as Consumer Assessment of Healthcare Providers and Systems (CAHPS). The CMS process requires that hospitals survey at least 300 patients annually if they wish to publicly report the results for comparative purposes on the CMS website, *www.hospitalcompare.gov*. The intent is to provide consumers with data from which to make decisions about the healthcare facilities they choose to seek care from. This could also intensify competition among healthcare facilities on relative service quality.

> ***"Paying for quality may become as important in the next 20 years as paying for case mix has been in the past 20 years."***
>
> —Kevin Quinn[1]

INCREASING COMPETITION AND MARKET DEMAND FOR SERVICE QUALITY

Competition has increased in all areas of healthcare. The moratorium on specialty hospitals will expire in 2006 and allow doctors and other entrepreneurs to continue the trend of creating facilities that have a singular focus on the more-profitable, less-complex elective surgeries. In the near future, competition will not be limited to these traditional healthcare players. U.S. consumers already spend upwards of $47 billion annually on alternative medicine therapies—acupuncture, massage therapists, chiropractors, and other service providers who have a *perceived* greater focus on the quality of service, not just the technical side of medicine.

Healthcare providers will also experience greater competition from traditional business firms. For example, Target Corporation just launched a 60-store pilot dubbed the "One-Minute Clinic." The clinic does only one thing—strep tests—but you get results in less than one minute. Target plans to cherry-pick the high-margin, technologically simple diagnostic tests that patients traditionally received in the doctor's office. Now, instead of waiting for an appointment, driving to the office, waiting in a cramped waiting room, waiting again in an exam room to see the doctor, and then waiting for the test results, you can do it while shopping for the comfort foods and cough drops that your strep throat requires. When highly successful service companies with massive customer bases, like Target, start entering the healthcare marketplace, it's time to watch out.

Underlying all of this is a fundamental shift toward consumer-driven healthcare where patients will pay a greater percent of their healthcare costs out-of-pocket. Health insurers are laying the foundation for high-deductible, high co-pay insurance plans that afford the patient maximum choice and information to use in order to self-select a healthcare provider. From December 2004 to June 2005, the number of enrollees in health savings accounts—a critical tool for consumer-driven healthcare—has doubled.

All predictions say that patients will be forced to pay more for and actually provide more of their own healthcare. Patients are already becoming more savvy and demanding, and the baby boomers, who have dominated and transformed every institution they have touched, can be expected to do the same in healthcare. As boomers increasingly enter healthcare facilities with illnesses or other healthcare needs, they will expect the service experience in healthcare to be at least as good as other experiences, if not better.

The pressure is on to compete, succeed, and win in a healthcare marketplace increasingly focused on clinical and service quality.

The intersection between clinical and service quality

Service recovery is about quality of service, not about quality of clinical care. Both should be of the highest quality, but sometimes we only focus on the clinical side of quality. Many healthcare professionals subconsciously think, "Our patients are patients, not customers. People come to our hospital because they're sick, not because they expect fine dining or six hundred-thread count sheets." No one will argue that saving lives is the first priority, however, that priority does not preclude providing high-quality service.

What's in a name?: Are they patients or customers?

"Patients," "customers," "residents," "clients," and other terms denoting a person receiving a service are used interchangeably. "Doctor," "physician," "nurse," "clinician," "staff," "employee," "volunteer," "associate," "provider," and other terms denoting a person delivering a service also are used interchangeably.

There is no consensus within the healthcare fields about terminology. Some insist that "patients" be used out of their deep emotional attachment to the word. Others insist that "customer" be used because "patients" are often treated paternalistically and as less than full persons. Also note that, in some instances, physicians can be seen as customers because they too partake of the services of a hospital and could, in most cases, choose to be on the staff of a different hospital.

Are they patients or customers?

Consultants often tell healthcare organizations that the key to service excellence is to "Stop calling them patients and start calling them customers." Not surprisingly, many healthcare professionals bristle at the suggestion. They may say things like, "Customers are fine at Saks Fifth Avenue, but we're not a department store," or "This isn't Burger King, and you can't have it your way in the hospital."

Yet healthcare consumers are, in fact, both patients and customers. Two emergency medicine physicians, Drs. Thomas Mayer and Robert Cates[2], who have conducted more than 150 healthcare customer service training programs, have found that when they asked their training audiences whether someone would be considered a patient or a customer, the answer depended on several factors.

What makes someone seem like a patient?
Patients were viewed as people who were acutely ill, dependent, and passive. Patients had less choice about being at the hospital, and staff felt that they were in control of the situation. Remember, healthcare professionals in general know how to take care of patients, many of whom are desperately ill and require timely, aggressive, and orderly interventions. Staff are trained to provide those clinical interventions and understand how to approach a patient.

What makes someone seem like a customer?
Customers were viewed as people who were not acutely ill and who were independent. Customers had a choice about being there—in other words, healthcare was a "discretionary purchase." Staff felt that the customers were in control of the situation. Many healthcare professionals don't know how to approach a "customer" who still has the technical healthcare needs but has much more power and control over the encounter than does the "patient." In fact, many people in healthcare may be uncomfortable talking about the "customer side of the equation."

Thus, a 55-year-old female brought to the emergency department (ED) by paramedics with an electrocardiogram and all other clinical indicators clearly showing that she is having myocardial infarction was always identified as a patient. However, a three-year-old child brought to the ED by his parents at 11:45 p.m. with a temperature of 99.2°, who were concerned because earlier that day their pediatrician diagnosed the boy with left otitis media, started him on antibiotics, and said to keep his fever down, was always identified as a customer (or, rather, the parents were seen as customers).

Are they patients or customers? (cont.)

A simple rule
Mayer and Cates created a rule to describe their observations. The more horizontal they are, the more they are a patient; the more vertical they are, the more they are a customer. Furthermore, this rating changes daily. For example, as the woman with the heart attack improves and becomes more "vertical," the staff may begin to realize that there are substantial customer features emerging through the course of her healthcare.

Who has higher expectations?
When Mayer and Cates ask their training audiences who had higher expectations, the woman with the heart attack or the parents of the child, the audience always says the parents—who were customers—would have higher expectations.

However, when asked what the woman with the heart attack wants, the audience always answers, "To live." When asked what the parents and child want, they answer, "Reassurance." Stated in this way, healthcare professionals begin to see that it's definitely odd to feel that someone who wants to live has *lower* expectations than someone who is just seeking reassurance.

This disconnect comes from the assumption that customers have high expectations, often because we don't know how to meet them when we haven't been explicitly trained how to do so. Conversely, acutely ill patients' expectations are rated low because the life-saving interventions are what the healthcare professional clearly knows how to deliver—and do so with pleasure and enthusiasm. Recognize and understand this tension in rating the expectations of the patient and the customer.

Both patient and customer, all the time
Staff need to understand that they have their own internal barometer of how they rate patients (and their families) on a daily basis. Many recognize that their internal rating system has been in effect for them forever. Rather than having the customer service training define for them what constitutes a patient or customer, the staff define it for themselves in a stunningly consistent fashion.

Thus, improving customer service is not a transition from patient to customer, which is often viewed as insulting or demeaning of healthcare professionals. Instead, it is a recognition that they are always both. Once healthcare organizations help their staff understand this dynamic, they have a substantial foundation for an excellent customer service program. Without it, the pragmatic side of customer service is difficult to enact.

We believe that the term used is less significant than showing affection and respect for everyone involved in the healthcare enterprise. We deeply respect all humans giving the profound gift of healthcare and have deep affection for all humans touched by illness. Please keep an open mind and apply the terms according to your own situation.

Clinical and service quality certainly overlap: Patients who get infections are less satisfied. We'd like to believe that making the right diagnoses, cutting in the right spots, delivering the right medicines, and calling it a day is all we need to do to get good clinical outcomes, but it isn't true. *How* we deliver that care matters almost as much as what we deliver. For example:

- When we discuss medication or therapy regimens with patients, we can simply say what needs to be said. Or we can package the education in ways that enhance patient understanding and recall, thereby increasing the likelihood of adherence.

- We can simply stick patients with IVs or insert catheters. Or we can introduce ourselves, talk in a reassuring manner, and answer questions while we do so.

- We can ignore patients' and families' distress. Or we can inquire about and address their emotional needs, thereby reducing stress and increasing their comfort.

- We can cut through patients' long explanations of their minor physical ailments and get to the point. Or, remembering that in the average patient-physician encounter doctors only allow patients 17 seconds before they interrupt, we can listen actively for the patient to fully describe their concerns before speaking.

Thus, although clinical quality is a necessary, minimum criterion, it is insufficient on its own. Patients want and deserve more.

The market is now providing the monetary incentives and opportunities to do more. But we can't simply tell staff to do more or try harder. Rather, we need to create systems that support staff in their efforts and set them up for success.

The mission

YOUR MISSION

Your mission is to contribute to the creation and execution of systems and processes that meet the goals of all your stakeholders: trustees/owners, employees, physicians, patients, and the

> *"Inferior care results when health professionals lack full mastery of their clinical areas or cannot communicate effectively and compassionately."*
>
> —Kathleen N. Lohr[3]

community. Although these constituents may have slightly different goals, all agree that we want a healthcare institution that survives and thrives by doing the good work of healing patients and families, creating healthier communities, providing genuinely fulfilling opportunities and a good work environment for employees, and creating a place for physicians to practice medicine to the fullest of their abilities.

Service recovery systems are established within the context of other systems used to reach these goals, typically a global service excellence or patient satisfaction strategic initiative. Of course, saying that something is of strategic importance does not necessarily mean that it us actually treated as if it's strategically important: Do as I say, not as I do, typically fails to create behavior change in any situation. Even in healthcare organizations, staff will imitate behaviors–especially those of leaders, managers, and supervisors. If they show that it is on their "radar," other staff will know it is important to the organization.

THE PRESS GANEY MISSION

Press Ganey can help you answer all of those questions. Our mission is to "partner with our clients in defining, assessing, and improving the quality of service to their customers." We're experts in applying rigorous psychometrics to measure what many consider unquantifiable. Each year, we survey more than nine million patients and help healthcare facilities use their customer data to improve their healthcare services. (The CD accompanying this book contains examples of Press Ganey patient satisfaction surveys and an explanation of our measurement scale.) Over the past five years, the customer revolution finally kicked in: The number of healthcare providers partnering with Press Ganey to measure satisfaction continuously has dramatically increased, from 1,564 in 2001 to more than 4,000 in 2005 (See Figure 1.1).

Figure 1.1

Number of healthcare facilities partnering with Press Ganey

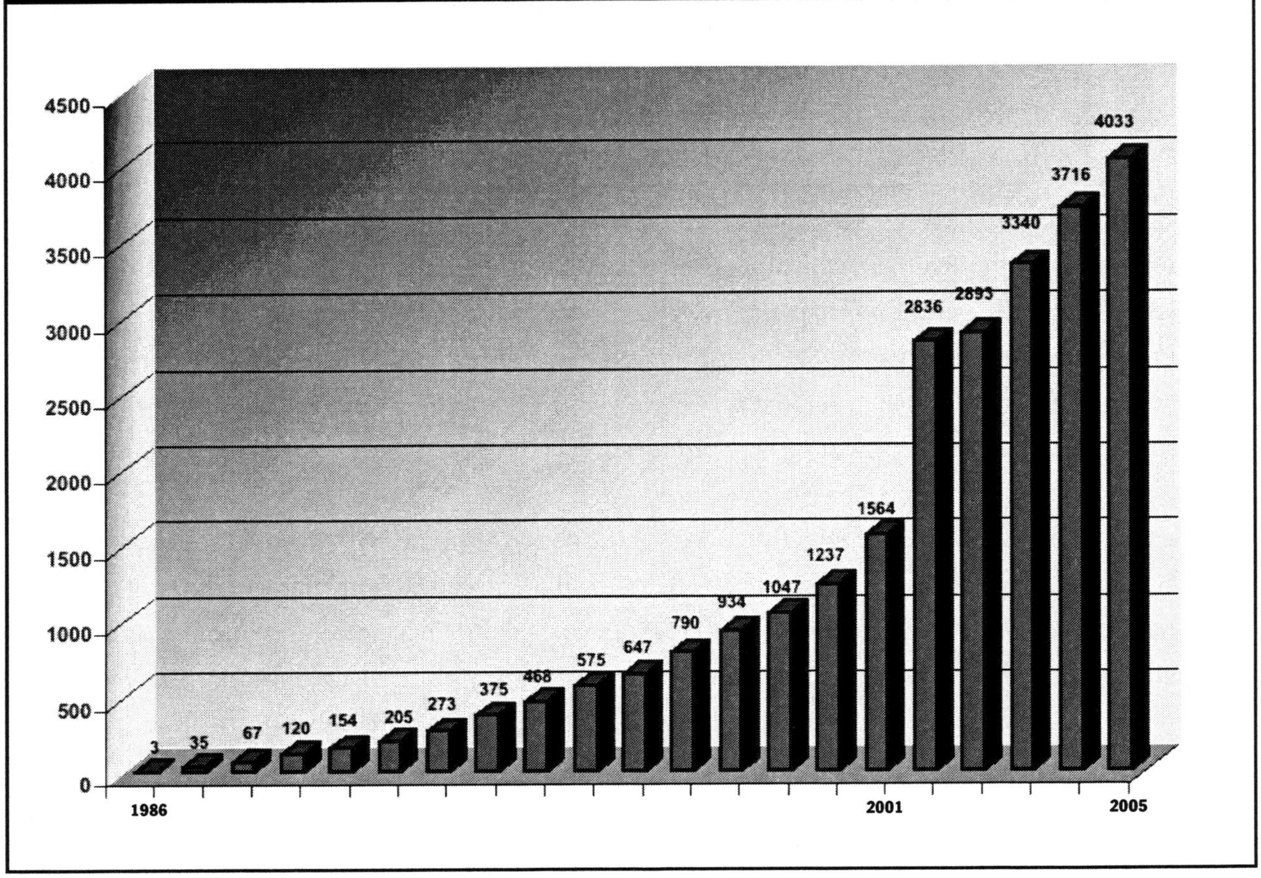

Facilities that have partnered with Press Ganey for the past five years have seen their overall patient satisfaction scores rise from 82.68 to 84.64 (as shown in Figure 1.2; note that the variation is consistent with normal seasonal variation). Note the contrast with the national average for hospitals, which the American Consumer Satisfaction Index found to have dropped to 70.8 in the first quarter of 2005 (from 76.0 in the first quarter of 2004). Similarly, the Kaiser Family Foundation, in conjunction with Harvard University and the Agency for Healthcare Research and Quality, conducted a nationwide phone survey published in late 2004 in which 55% of those surveyed said that they were dissatisfied with the quality of healthcare, up from 44% in 2000—and 40% said the quality of care had gotten worse in the past five years.

Figure 1.2

Overall mean score by discharge month

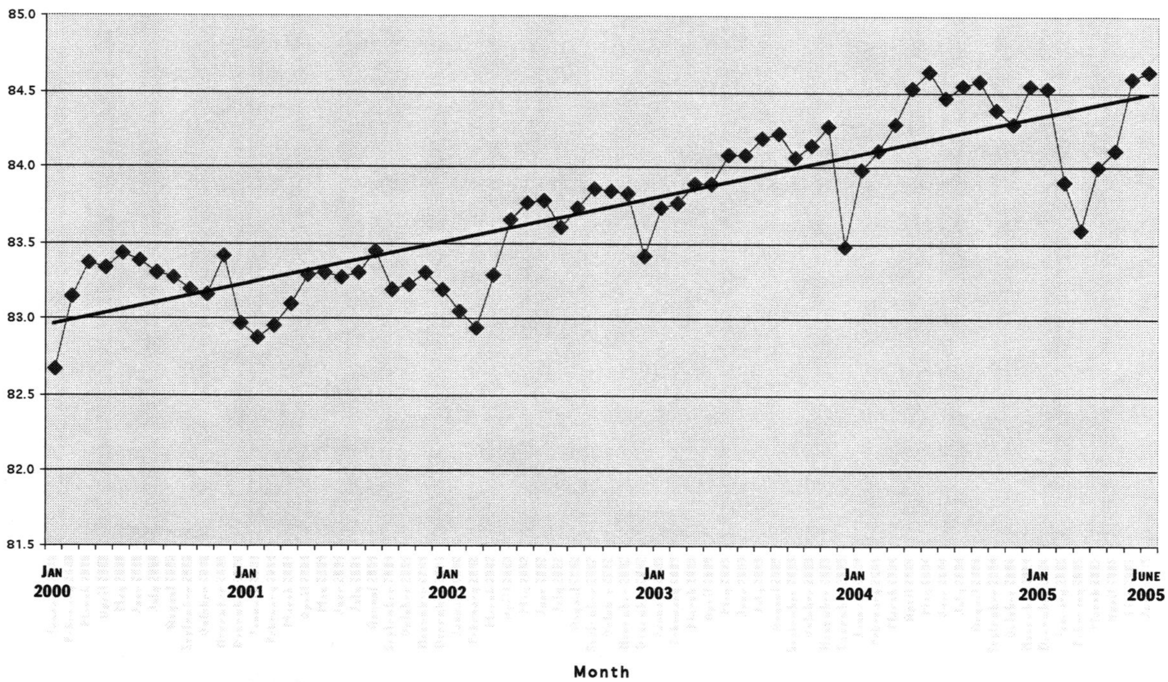

Healthcare organizations partnering with Press Ganey also dominate healthcare quality awards and rankings, such as Solucient's Top 100 hospitals, *Fortune* magazine's best employers, Consumer Choice awards, Magnet hospitals, and Malcolm Baldrige National Quality award.

Because we provide a systematic performance measurement and management system for satisfaction, we enable our partners to focus on improvement instead of on the nitty-gritty details of managing the measurement, reporting, and feedback processes. A recent study found that having such a system is predictive of high performance in healthcare quality improvement:

> We identified some key characteristics that separated the high performing from the low performing groups . . . Groups that encouraged formal involvement in quality improvement, such as implementing a systematic method of measuring patient satisfaction and a requirement to report quality results to outside bodies, were more likely to rank in the top 25 percent of almost all performance measures.[4]

Endnotes

1. Kevin Quinn, "Dividing a trillion-dollar pie," *Healthcare Financial Management* 58, no. 4 (April 2004): 60.

2. Thomas A. Mayer and Robert J. Cates, "Are they patients or are they customers?," *The Satisfaction Monitor* (July/Aug 1998).

3. Kathleen N. Lohr, "How do we measure quality?," *Health Affairs* 16, no. 3 (May/June 1997): 7–21.

4. Stephen M. Shortell, Julie Schmittdiel, Margaret C. Wang, et al, "An empirical assessment of high-performing medical groups: Results from a national study," *Medical Care Research and Review* 62, no. 4 (Aug 1 2005): 407–434.

CHAPTER 2

INTRODUCING SERVICE RECOVERY

Matt Davis, Katie Drevs, Peggy Fuerbringer,
Michelle Gloss, Deborah Spite

The overworked nurse and challenging patient

The following is a true story; only the names have been changed. On a skiing vacation far from home, Jean Pierre broke his leg and was brought to the local hospital. The emergency department (ED) was in the midst of a huge influx of patients, many of whom were in critical condition, and Mr. Pierre had to wait for hours. During that time, the pain medication he was given barely touched the discomfort from his bruised muscles and broken bone. By the time he was finally admitted, he felt neglected, not cared for, and hungry.

As he settled into a private room, he was greeted by his nurse, Beth Williams, who was just starting hour 11 of a 12-hour shift. Nonetheless, she managed to smile and quietly asked whether there was anything she could do to make his stay more comfortable.

Pierre, a man who never missed an opportunity to speak his mind or force people to live up to their promises, delivered this response:

"I'll tell you what you can do for me. I missed dinner, and I'm starving, and not for one of your wimpy hospital meals. I want a big steak, medium rare, and a baked potato with butter—not margarine, butter." And then he sat back in his bed, folded his arms across his chest, and stared down the exhausted nurse.

Williams remembered all the talk about mission, patient satisfaction, and service excellence, but she was already exhausted, so she only replied that she would see what she could do. Back at the nurses' station, Williams described this challenging patient to her manager, who nodded sympathetically, remembering her own many difficult patients when she was on the floor. The manager knew that Williams' shift was almost over, but she also understood the value of employee empowerment, so she asked Williams what she would like to do about the situation.

"Actually, I'd really like to get him that steak and potato. Maybe if he sees that we can come through with a request like that, he won't be so hard on the third shift tonight."

The manager okayed the ambitious deed, and Williams made a run to the local supermarket. Next the head cook took on the task of preparing the meal to the patient's specifications. An orderly delivered the steak and potato to Pierre immediately, with a side of real butter.

Pierre was surprised and delighted and effusively thanked Williams and everyone else involved. For the rest of his life, he made good on is promise to tell everyone he knew about his amazing experience at the hospital.

What is service recovery?

Service recovery is about making things right after something goes wrong. It can be as simple as apologizing or as complicated as orchestrating an entire meal for one patient, and it salvages the customer relationship by regaining trust and building loyalty.

There are three steps to each individual act of service recovery:

1. Recognizing that something went wrong
2. Apologizing
3. Taking action and making amends

Recognizing that something went wrong

The first step is to recognize that something went wrong and that a patient's expectations were not met. The thing that went wrong can be as simple as forgetting to bring a blanket to a patient or responding late to a call bell—things that, in the hustle bustle of today's busy world, staff might not even identify as something that went wrong.

People respond in a variety of ways when something doesn't meet their expectations. Some of us complain. Complaints make it is easy to recognize a service failure, but only a small number of people complain, and they usually only do so to a front-line employee. If that front-line employee cannot resolve the issue, an even smaller percentage will file a formal written complaint or grievance using the official process. In addition, the majority of us say nothing to anyone at the service provider.

Nevertheless, we do talk. Many will say something to family, friends, neighbors and colleagues—and what we say is not good word-of-mouth advertising. Others, depending upon their options and the perceived severity of the service failure, decide not to return to that provider. In the worst-case scenario, the provider fails to meet expectations for both service expectations and clinical outcomes, which makes patients or their families more likely to sue.

Thus, the first crucial step in an individual act of service recovery is to recognize the "oops," at the moment it occurred, or very soon thereafter, regardless of whether the patient says anything about it then or ever.

Put yourself in the patient's place

What would I do if my loved one was admitted to the hospital today?

Would I want to see them?
Would I want to be with them?
Would I want to stay the night?
Would I bring food, blankets, books or other comfort items?
Would I call other family or friends?

What would I want to know?

The diagnosis? The prognosis?
What medications have been given?
How long they will have to stay here?
Whether they will be able to do all the things they used to do?
What my role is? What I will have to help with? What this will mean for our life?

What concerns would be running through my mind?

Who is paying for this?
How will we afford this?

Apologizing

The second crucial part is, of course, the recovery after the service failure. This process begins with a sincere apology. Apologies communicate the important message of understanding. By apologizing, you share in the customer's experience—which is not the same as accepting blame. In the blameless apology, the apology and empathy are about the fact that the patient experienced the unpleasant incident—as in, "I'm sorry you went through that. That must have been difficult. I care that you're upset. I want to help you feel better." (Scripts for delivering sincere, blameless apologies are included in the CD that accompanies this book.)

"Tsze-Kung asked, 'Is there one word which may serve as a rule of practice for all one's life?' The Master said, 'Is not Reciprocity such a word? What you do not want done to yourself, do not do to others.' "

—Confucius (551–479 B.C.)
from Lun Yu, *The Analects of Confucius,* Legge XV 23

Taking action and making amends

A sincere apology is just the beginning: It helps assuage any immediate anger and allows you to work together to find a solution that meets or exceeds expectations. Service providers in any industry can make it right by fulfilling the service promised and expected.

Also note that people often have an innate psychological sense of fairness or justice that is violated when a promise has been broken or when time or money is lost. Although it will not fix the problem, offering something to acknowledge the failure to meet their expectations can help you regain their trust. It can make the wronged person feel that a large institution cares about them.

For example, to balance the emotional ledger of a minor service failure, you can offer a $10.00 gift certificate, parking passes, movie tickets, or free dinner at a popular restaurant. (Examples of gift certificates and other such tokens are contained in the CD that accompanies this book.) If the service failure was more significant, a straight check or gift certificate for use at a store to replace the lost item would be appropriate.

Recognizing the wrong and making it right through apology, action, and reciprocity all must occur immediately—on the front line, by the person who has recognized the oops. This is the "moment of truth" where patients find out exactly who and what they are dealing with—a giant, impersonal, inflexible bureaucracy, or a group of people who really care about them.

Part II

Philosophy

CHAPTER 3

REGULATIONS AND STANDARDS GOVERNING COMPLAINTS

Matt Davis, Katie Drevs, Peggy Fuerbringer,
Michelle M. Gloss, Deborah Spite

Introduction

Four sets of standards address handling complaints in healthcare: the Centers for Medicaid & Medicare Services (CMS), the Joint Commission on Accreditation of Healthcare Organizations (JCAHO), the International Organization for Standardization (ISO), and the Malcolm Baldrige National Quality Award criteria.

CMS CONDITIONS OF PARTICIPATION

Today, any hospital in the United States that wants to be able to bill Medicare and Medicaid for its services must have a grievance and complaint policy and procedure in place. That's because the newly adopted CMS Conditions of Participation (CoP)[1] regulations require facilities to have a "process for prompt resolution of patient grievances that has been approved by the hospital's governing board."

The CoP Interpretative Guidelines explain what CMS expects (see Appendix A for the complete text of the interpretive guidelines). They require healthcare facilities to

- Establish a process, approved by the hospital's governing body, for prompt resolution of patient grievances.
- Have the governing body review and resolve grievances, unless it delegated that responsibility, in writing, to a grievance committee.
- Inform patients whom to contact to file a grievance (including a phone number and address).
- Inform patients that they may lodge a grievance with the state licensure agency directly, regardless of whether they use the hospital grievance procedure.
- Specify time frames for review of the grievance and provision of a written response

(note that if the grievance is complicated and the investigation will not be completed within seven days, the hospital must so inform the patient or the patient's representative and state when the hospital will follow up).

- Describe how to refer the issue to the quality improvement organization (QIO).
- Describe the review process, steps taken on the patient's behalf, notification of the results, and information on who to contact with questions.
- Provide an appeals process.

JCAHO REQUIREMENTS

The JCAHO also requires that healthcare facilities have a process to handle patient complaints. The Elements of Performance to Standard RI.2.120 require that a hospital

- Inform patients, families, and staff about the complaint resolution process.
- Receive, review, and, when possible, resolve complaints from patients and their families.
- Respond to individuals making what the hospital defines as a significant or recurring complaint.
- Inform patients that they have the right to file a complaint with the state authority.

The standard further notes that patients should be able to freely voice complaints and recommend changes without being subject to coercion, discrimination, reprisal, or unreasonable interruption of care, treatment, and services.

THE INTERNATIONAL ORGANIZATION FOR STANDARDIZATION

The ISO is a network of national standards institutes of 156 countries. Multinational corporations typically seek ISO certification so that their international customers can be assured that certain quality standards are being met. Most healthcare organizations are not international in scope, and thus few seek ISO certification. Nonetheless, because ISO standards represent a broad international consensus, it is useful to look at the ISO standard for complaints handling (ISO 10002).

Among other things, ISO 10002 sets forth some guiding principles for how processes for handling complaints should be built. They include the following:

Accessibility: the public must know how to complain. As a rule of thumb, the more formal the system for lodging complaints, the less accessible it is to consumers.

Accountability: someone in the organization must be responsible for handling complaints.

Customer-focused approach: an organization that adopts a customer-focused approach invites complaints and indicates commitment to resolving complaints through its words and actions.

Fairness and objectivity: the complaint should be judged on its merits, and there should be fairness to all concerned.

Free-of-charge and confidential: the process should be free of charge to complainants and maintain appropriative confidentiality.

Responsiveness: complaints need to be dealt with quickly. The more quickly the complaints are addressed, the higher the customer satisfaction.

Visibility: the public has to know where to complain. It might be obvious in a small, one-premise operation, but it is not in the case of a large multi-site organization.

ISO 10002 also explains why organizations should commit to effective complaints-handling and describes considerations for developing, planning, and designing a complaints-handling policy. It provides guidance for operating the process—from receiving a complaint through closing the issue after completion. It also outlines how to gather and use complaints data, monitoring performance of the complaints-handling process, auditing the process to ensure that it meets the organization's requirements, and improving it continually.

MALCOLM BALDRIGE NATIONAL QUALITY AWARD CRITERIA

The Malcolm Baldrige National Quality Award (MBNQA) was established by Congress in 1987. It came about in part because U.S. leadership in product and process quality was being fiercely challenged by foreign competition, and the country's productivity growth had improved less than its competitors' over the previous two decades.

The MBNQA program promulgates a set of criteria used to evaluate the organization during site visits. The healthcare industry had its first winner in 2002. The four healthcare winners—Robert Wood Johnson University Hospital Hamilton, Baptist Hospital, Inc., St. Luke's Hospital of Kansas City, and SSM Healthcare—are all Press Ganey partners. All four measured patient and employee satisfaction using survey questions such as "response to concerns/complaints."

The MBNQA criteria do not mandate specific practices. Instead, the applicant organizations must present the practices, processes, or policies they used to achieve the values and concepts set forth in the criteria (see Appendix B). A recent study found that service recovery was among the most frequently used best practices among all Baldrige Award winners.[2] Another recent study empirically demonstrated that service recovery and related leadership activities are critical components in achieving the high process quality needed to meet the MBNQA criteria.[3]

Baseline responsibilities for a formal grievance process

The standards discussed above represent the consensus of what healthcare policymakers consider to be the minimum necessary to ensure basic healthcare quality. Although your facility may not be required to comply with all of these standards, it is clear that handling patient complaints is something that must be done.

With that in mind, consider the following baseline responsibilities for a formal complaint process in healthcare.

1. Have the board delegate responsibility for the process to a grievance committee

Remember that the CMS CoP expects the hospital's governing board to approve and be responsible for the operation of the grievance process and to review and resolve grievances, unless it delegates its responsibility, in writing, to a grievance committee. Get that delegation and establish a multidisciplinary committee that will report to the board of directors. This multidisciplinary committee will be responsible for crafting the complaint/grievance policy and administering the review process. (See Chapter 8 for more information.)

Ownership of this responsibility varies among institutions. In some hospitals, it may lie with risk management or quality improvement. Others may place it with safety, patient services, service excellence, or patient relations.

2. Communicate the formal process to patients

Patients must know to whom they can complain, how the complaint will be handled, and whether it will be taken seriously. Generally this information is included as part of the Patient Rights materials given to patients at admission.This information can be further emphasized and communicated by doing one of the following:

- Post the process and contact information on the organization's Web site
- Place copies in the patient's room

- Place copies in the patient's chart
- Include it in the discharge materials
- Place concise brochures at strategic locations such as waiting rooms, entrances, or nurses' stations (see Appendix C for a sample brochure; the CD that accompanies this book contains other samples)
- Place attractive posters on the walls of patients' room to inspire excellence from staff

3. Triage: Is it a complaint or a grievance?

Complaints must be evaluated to ascertain whether they trigger a facility's *formal* grievance process. Here are some basic rules of thumb based on the CMS CoP guidelines:

- When the patient *requests* the issue be handled as a formal complaint/grievance, it's a grievance.

- When staff encounter a complaint or concern that is deferred to others for further investigation or resolution *at a later period in time* (e.g., more than one day), it's a formal grievance.

- A written complaint is *always* considered a grievance. If someone takes the time and effort to write to your organization, consider their complaint a significant issue worthy of your diligent attention in the formal grievance process. This includes *attachments* to patient satisfaction surveys. Note, however, survey comments are *not* grievances if they could have been resolved at the time the patient was hospitalized, that is, if the patient complained or voiced the concern while in the hospital.

- E-mail and fax complaints are considered written complaints. You may respond via e-mail pursuant to your policy.

- Survey comments are not grievances unless a quality-of-care issue is raised by the respondent. An automated program, such as Press Ganey's *Hot Comments,* can allow you to set keywords that identify and automatically notify you of patient comments severe enough to qualify as formal grievances.

- Billing issues are not grievances unless they are from a Medicare beneficiary regarding rights and limitations provided by law.

- Telephone complaints are handled like any other complaint. For example, if post-discharge callbacks encounter patient complaints, document and address them through the formal grievance/complaint procedure.

- Severe circumstances, such as alleged abuse, neglect, patient harm, or hospital compliance with CMS regulations, are always considered formal grievances.

4. All voiced concerns or complaints must be resolved

Any employee present when a patient voices a complaint, as well as anyone in a position designed to respond to the issue implicit in the complaint (e.g., maintenance, housekeeping, food services, patient advocates, etc.) must resolve the complaint in a reasonable time frame. Remember, the CMS considers complaints that cannot be resolved at the time of the complaint to be grievances.

5. When the patient is satisfied, the grievance is resolved

Patient expectations and the response necessary for compliance should be "appropriate and reasonable." In our earlier story, if Mr. Pierre's nurse had brought him the standard box meal from food services, she would have fulfilled the minimum duty. But, of course, this action would not have won a raving fan, nor would it create a legendary story in their hospital to serve as inspiration for everyone.

There may be situations where the hospital has taken appropriate and reasonable actions on the patient's behalf in order to resolve the patient's grievance and the patient or the patient's representative remains unsatisfied with the hospital's actions. In these situations the hospital may consider the grievance closed for the purposes of these requirements. The hospital must maintain documentation of its efforts and demonstrate compliance with CMS requirements.

6. The formal grievance process must include information on how to report issues to the appropriate QIO

This includes notifying patients of their rights to appeal premature discharge or lodge a complaint regarding quality of care. The Quality Improvement Organization (QIO) complaint process and its coordination with the hospital's formal grievance process must be explained.

7. Designate a time frame for which all issues must be addressed

Seven days is the average time frame within which the CMS requires a response. Occasionally, a grievance is complicated and may require an extensive investigation. Moreover, staff scheduling and fluctuations in the numbers and complexity of grievances can affect the time frames for the provision of written responses. Therefore, although CMS considers seven days the average time frame for grievance resolution, they recognize grievances often take longer and set forth steps to follow if it remains unresolved.

If the grievance will not be resolved, or if the investigation cannot be completed within seven days, the hospital should inform the patient or the patient's representative that the hospital is still working to resolve the grievance and that the hospital will follow up with a written response within a stated number of days in accordance with each hospital's grievance policy. The hospital must attempt to resolve all grievances as soon as possible.

8. The board of directors must review and approve the entire formal grievance process

As noted earlier, CMS requires the highest authorities to have operational knowledge of the standard procedure for handling formal complaints regarding clinical or service quality.

9. Include the review of other quality of care indicators as part of your service quality improvement program

Doing so provides good supplementary information to indicate areas on which to focus improvement resources and attention. Be able to show what other areas you are gathering information about to identify service problems, such as

- patient survey comments
- post-discharge phone calls
- employee and medical staff surveys and comments
- service-oriented culture survey
- safety culture survey
- suggestion boxes
- patient interviews
- patient focus groups

Note that, although gathering this information provides you with specific direction on where to focus improvement efforts, these assessments, in and of themselves, do not improve satisfaction. For example, Barnes-Jewish Hospital used patient advocates to conduct many pre-discharge patient interviews. The patient advocate identified many service quality problems but failed to improve patient satisfaction during the 12-week study period. The lack of improvement might have occurred because the advocate simply reported the problem to a nurse or nursing supervisor and assumed no responsibility for service improvements or recovery efforts. It also might have been because there was no systematic service recovery effort. Either way, the point is simple: Measurement or assessment alone isn't enough to generate improvement.[4]

10. Track and trend complaints and service recovery activities

Tracking and trending is crucial to any successful service recovery program. This means tracking and trending both complaints/grievances *and* service recovery activities. Access® databases or Excel® spreadsheets sometimes are the most effective and simple. The CD in this workbook provides an example of a basic tracking mechanism in Excel. Off-the-shelf commercial software is also available, and programs such as RL Solutions or Customer Expressions can integrate with, and automate, other risk-management activities.

You need to be able to trend complaints over time by different classifications and in different departments, functional areas, and service lines. These data can be used to hold managers accountable for service quality in their areas. Elimination or reduction in complaints over time is not required. Complaints may, in fact, increase as you improve your complaint-gathering process. Rather than eliminate complaints, you must show that you've recognized that you've received many complaints regarding a certain issue and that you've done something about it. Your quality improvement documentation (e.g., action plans, intervention designs, post-mortem analyses, etc.) will all serve this purpose. Note also that the CMS requires all complaint/grievance documentation to be housed in a central location.

11. Assess the effectiveness of your grievance process

The common approach for assessing the effectiveness of traditional complaint management is to track the number of complaints per 1,000 patients. However, this metric may be misleading. Complaint rates depend upon your definition of a complaint and the quality of your complaint management processes.

Your complaint rate will be determined by the system you've created for filing formal written complaints and tracking complaints. If the process is not customer-friendly your complaint rate will be lower—but so will your inherent service quality, satisfaction, and word-of-mouth reputation. As you establish your service recovery system and encourage customer feedback, the number of complaints often increases—but so will your customer satisfaction and loyalty.

Making things more difficult, there is no national average or accepted minimum for complaint rates in healthcare. The rates quoted below are based on reported studies. (See

Appendix D for a complete list of studies, rates, and how to calculate rates.)

For those who define a complaint as any complaint written in a letter or that follows the formal complaint/grievance process, (that is, the CMS definition), rates reported vary between a low of 0.6/1,000 to 6.2/1,000. On the other hand, those who have an expanded definition of a complaint to include any verbal complaint made to a healthcare professional or on a survey report much higher rates, as much as 50–100/1,000) for the healthcare industry.

Some organizations make statistical adjustments to reflect such things as staff-patient ratio or nurse-patient ratio. Frankly, however, this method is messy and can be time-consuming. You should be spending most of your time doing something about the complaints, not forever tweaking the numbers.

What matters most is that patient complaints are resolved to patients' satisfaction, so measure that instead. It doesn't really matter whether the number of complaints goes up or down if your patients' *satisfaction* and *loyalty* increases.

Always remember that the key determinants of whether patients formally complain include their overall satisfaction with your services, their satisfaction with staff response to their verbal concerns and complaints, how effectively you communicate the process to patients, and the extent to which your formal complaint process is customer-friendly. A low complaint rate does not mean that your patients do not have complaints.

How effective is your grievance process?

Are patients'/patient representatives' concerns addressed in a timely manner?

Are patients informed of any resolution to their grievances?

Does the hospital apply what it learns from the grievance as part of its continuous quality improvement activities?

Endnotes

1. Centers for Medicare & Medicaid Services. Conditions of Participation. Interpretative Guidelines, S&C-05-42; August 18, 2005. Available from: *http://www.cms.hhs.gov/medicaid/survey-cert/sc0542.pdf*; Accessed: October 28, 2005.

2. Susan West Engelkemeyer and Kathleen Seiders, "Creating Value and Stakeholder Benefits: Customer-Focused Practices of Baldrige Award Recipients" (paper, 2003 Production Operations Management Society Conference: The Service Economy, Savannah, GA, April 4–7, 2003).

3. Kathyrn A. Marley, David A. Collier, and Susan Meyer Goldstein, "The role of clinical and process quality in achieving patient satisfaction in hospitals," *Decision Sciences* 35, no. 3 (June 2004): 349–69.

4. Jane Garbutt, Diana Bose, Beth A. McCawley, Tom Burroughs, and Gerald Medoff, "Soliciting patient complaints to improve performance," *Joint Commission Journal on Quality and Patient Safety* 29, no. 3 (March 2003): 103–12.

Part III

Process

CHAPTER 4

BEYOND REGULATORY COMPLIANCE:

A SERVICE EXCELLENCE STRATEGY TO ENHANCE EMPLOYEE, PATIENT, AND PHYSICIAN LOYALTY

Authors: Matt Davis, Katie Drevs,
Peggy Fuerbringer, Michelle Gloss, Deborah Spite

You and your organization have a choice: simply meet regulatory standards or seek true excellence in service. Service excellence can be defined as being prepared for service failure at the same time that you are striving to get it right the first time. The fact that you are reading this book means you have probably already made your own personal choice.

High patient satisfaction with your facility's response to concerns and complaints reduces complaints, formal grievances, and malpractice liability. It also increases productivity, employee job satisfaction, employee and patient loyalty, and positive word-of-mouth. The challenge is to create a system that helps you consistently change negative experiences into positive ones.

To achieve service excellence, a service recovery program must be seamlessly integrated into the daily business of healthcare delivery. It's not an extra or add-on objective, and it's not just the leaders, champions, and superstars who must make it happen—it's everyone. Effective service recovery systems change the way everyone on staff automatically and consistently reacts to certain situations.

Service excellence combines with and enhances customer satisfaction efforts, continuous quality improvement (CQI) initiatives, and the organization's mission and values. For example, if one of your CQI efforts is to increase appointment compliance, you can do so by reclaiming disaffected patients through an active service recovery program—which will simultaneously increase patient satisfaction, increase the likelihood of a better health outcome, and help staff feel better about the service they provide.

The 1996 national review: Best practices for resolving customer complaints

In 1996, in response to a presidential executive order, the federal government conducted a benchmarking study to determine best practice standards for resolving customer complaints.[1] The study benchmarked public and private businesses doing the best job of customer complaint resolution. It then determined why they were the best and what specific actions made could be transferred to any business. Their recommendations are as valuable now as they were then. (See box on pages 36 and 37 for a complete list.)

Customer orientation: A necessary shared value

In their ground-breaking study of successful American companies, *In Search of Excellence,* Tom Peters and Robert Waterman discovered that excellence began with shared values. One value held by all high-performing companies in their study (and by healthcare organizations in our study) was customer-orientation.

When a plurality of the organization's members truly values customer service, it becomes unmistakable. They are not just paying it lip service; they are applying it to the actual lived experience. In such an environment, patient expressions of worry, concern, or disappointment are no longer seen as an annoyance or burden. Rather, they become *service recovery opportunities*. People who value customer service look for the chance to show what they can do to help someone out. Service excellence becomes a reality when you have systems in place to support and encourage such efforts.

Synergizing, or achieving multiple goals through one organizational change or improvement effort, is essential in today's healthcare environment. Any new program or initiative is in danger of becoming just one more responsibility piling into an ever-growing inbox. It can be a daunting challenge not only to find the time yourself but also to convince your senior executives to spend the money and motivate front-line staff to participate. This job isn't just big—it's huge.

TAKE A SYSTEMS VIEW

The healthcare world is full of large, complex organizations. Achieving anything long-term begins with taking a systems view and with fundamentally changing the underlying organizational culture. To do so, ask the following questions:

- Are the employees, managers, and executives in your organization oriented toward service excellence?
- What are their reactions to hearing patients' complaints?
- Have you spoken with them, one-on-one, and really listened to understand their views?
- Does service excellence really matter to them?
- How do they react to patient dissatisfaction and complaints?

To avoid grievances, an organization must act, not react. Front-line staff must monitor situations constantly to identify problems. Patient advocates and service recovery agents of the organization must do rounds, and know how to read the body language of patients/residents. Approaching patients and their families to identify problems that they are experiencing, but have not voiced, is one of the best opportunities to "wow" your customers. Imagine the relief for your patients/residents when they realize that their complaints will not elicit retaliation, proven by the mere fact that you are encouraging them to voice their concerns.

Service recovery is not just about mistakes, however. You also must actively solicit customer desires, concerns, and complaints in order to keep up with shifts in market demand. The best way to do so is to embed an organized service recovery system in a culture that not only adeptly transforms service failures but also zealously seeks out all customer feedback.

Healthcare organizations are run by people and, as we know, "to err is human." Service recovery gives the patient the opportunity to "be divine"—that is, to forgive. Most people can be very forgiving of mistakes, if the mistakes are handled appropriately. Acknowledging mistakes and making an effort to fix them is often all it takes to turn a bad experience into a good one.

MAKE IT EASY TO COMPLAIN

It's not all that surprising to find out that patients are more loyal when their complaints are resolved effectively, but it is somewhat surprising to find out that they are also more loyal when they simply voice their complaints. Whether a loyal patient feels more comfortable complaining or the ease of complaining creates a loyal patient is unknown. Either

National best practice standards for resolving customer complaints

Five recommendations

1. Make it easy for your customers to complain and your customers will make it easy for you to improve.

The best-in-business want their customers to complain: Informed customers know how your services should work, and if things are not working, customers are the first to know. In addition, customers who are dissatisfied tell twice as many people about their experience as do those who are happy with your service. The best-in-business use feedback from calls to free hotlines, letters, and surveys to identify and resolve root causes of dissatisfaction and to change their services so that the customer will be satisfied quickly.

2. Respond to complaints quickly, courteously, and with common sense to improve customer loyalty.

Customers reward companies that solve problems quickly by remaining loyal customers. A speedy response can add 25% to customer loyalty. Toyota Motor Sales USA, Inc., has adopted the following formula for customer satisfaction:

Doing the job right the first time
\+ Effective complaint management
= Maximum customer satisfaction/loyalty

3. Resolve complaints on the first contact to (1) save money by eliminating unnecessary additional contacts that escalate costs and (2) build customer confidence.

A call back that involves two or more employees costs more than a call that is handled right the first time. Indeed, in this national study, resolving a complaint on the first contact reduced the cost by at least 50%.

4. The use of technology is critical in complaint-handling systems.

Use your computers to develop a database of complaints. Look for a trend, and if you find one, fix it. The study found that the best-in-business electronically compiled customer

National best practice standards for resolving customer complaints (cont.)

complaint information and presented it to everyone, including management, so that the organization could better align services and products to meet customer expectations.

5. Recruit and hire the best for customer service jobs.
The customer service and complaint resolution specialist positions established by benchmarking partners tend to be highly sought-after. Complaint specialists learn the company so well that they get promoted. Some organizations build the customer service position into a formal career ladder for advancement in the company. In all instances, front-line employees were valued for feedback in making decisions.

Five steps to a first-rate complaint system with results within six months

1. Issue a policy statement that says your organization embraces complaints and views complaints as opportunities.

2. Establish an implementation team.
Include on the team representatives from any department or management level that would be involved in or responsible for any step in the complaint-handling process.

3. Establish a tracking system.
Your staff should record and classify complaints, which will allow them to analyze the complaint data and report to top management. The difference between your process and the best-in-business process is known as the gap. A gap analysis will show you what to improve.

4. Develop recommendations to improve your core processes and to empower front-line employees to resolve complaints on first contact.

5. Implement it.
Put together an action plan for implementing the approved recommendations.

way, simply encouraging complaints is an effective measure. Add to that speedy service recovery and you can significantly enhance "customers' perception of the quality of the . . . services . . . as well as their perception of the competence of the organization and its personnel. This also enhances the perceived quality and value of other products and services the organization offers."[2]

It is not always easy for patients to complain to someone in a healthcare facility. Research has shown that consumers of medical care are more likely to engage in negative word-of-mouth than they are to complain directly to their healthcare provider.[3] They also may be intimidated by the doctors and nurses, fear jeopardizing the existing relationship, or fear affecting future care they might need.[4]

Thus, it falls to the healthcare provider to make complaining as easy as possible. It is also of utmost importance that the complaint process comes with a guarantee that there will never be any redress. It is not enough to have a plan in place, you also must advertise that you welcome complaints and concerns. More importantly, show that the complaints will be accepted happily and without retaliation.

View complaints as a gift

Few people associate the word "complaint" with anything positive. Typically, people think that a complaint means something went wrong because somebody did something wrong. Complaints are associated with negative feedback or punishment. In reality, however, complaints are a gift—they deliver a clear message as to how to improve service, delivered by the very people for whom we wish to do so.[5] Without complaints, a healthcare organization may be unaware that certain problems even exist. Complaints provide a wealth of market intelligence, free of charge.

Every successful organization understands the importance of feedback from customers, and most of the time that feedback comes in the form of complaints. They often come complete with the answer to the problem they identify. For example, all of the following real complaints came with a suggested response:

- The room was facing the interior of the hospital. All I could see from the window was the dirt and trash that blew around. My visitors also noticed. Why not clean the area up and put some local artist sculptures there?

- I had to park so far away. They should provide a free shuttle to the hospital.

- It would have been nice if someone had told us that the radiology department was running behind schedule.

- The food service person had obviously just come back from a smoke break. She should have washed her hands before returning to work.

Convincing the decision-makers: What is the return-on-investment?

Your organization may already have made a commitment to service excellence and service recovery. You may already have a mission statement in place that reflects that commitment, and front-line staff and top-level management may already be out there walking the walk and talking the talk. However, many organizations are not quite at that point and need to convince those with the power to say "yea" or "nay" to creation of a service recovery program.

Some of the most common reasons decision-makers deny a request for a service recovery program include the following:

- Our employees don't have the time to worry about a service recovery program. They are complaining that there aren't enough nurses, and they are already burdened with patient satisfaction. This is just one more thing they don't have time to do.

- Our physicians only care about the clinical quality of patient care. They won't see a service recovery program as improving patient care because that's not what's important to them.

- Our patients come here because of our clinical outcomes, and we have some of the best in the area.

- Service recovery programs cost money, but they don't bring money in. If there's anything left, we can look into a service recovery program.

But the facts show that these reasons lack substance. Service recovery programs, as part of an overall satisfaction measurement program, can help the bottom line.

The importance of service recovery to the bottom line

Service recovery systems are indispensable to achieving excellence in the delivery of health services. Service recovery is necessary because service failure is inevitable. There will always be mistakes, unmet expectations, or unexpected circumstances, no matter how well your services perform. And as the healthcare marketplace becomes increasingly competitive, achieving excellent results in patient satisfaction becomes increasingly predictive of business success.

Patient loyalty

On a certain level, the importance of patient loyalty is obvious—loyal patients will return for their future healthcare needs. Moreover, retaining a customer is far less expensive than finding a new one to take that customer's place.

Think beyond the immediate present. You want to be there when your former patient considers elective surgery, looks for a primary care physician, recommends a hospital to a friend or daughter to give birth, fills prescriptions, etc. In fact, research indicates that healthcare customers rely on information provided by family and friends more than any other source of information about the quality of healthcare at an organization.[6]

Building patient loyalty almost always requires service recovery strategies. Today, an *expectation of service recovery* has evolved, and healthcare organizations must be prepared to do the same. For more than a decade, many restaurants have regularly offered customers a free dessert when there are long waits for a table. Market-savvy consumers now expect to receive free coupons, reimbursements, forgiven fees, and free additional services after they complain. If your healthcare organization fails to prevent or resolve customer problems, you disappoint the customer twice: once for the initial failure and once for failing to correct what went wrong. When immediate action and planned responsiveness to service failure occurs, organizations are able to retain up to 95% of their dissatisfied customers.[7]

When healthcare organizations handle problems promptly and effectively, the expectation of action is fulfilled and loyalty captured. In addition to strengthening the bond between patient and healthcare provider, satisfying patients on the spot (that is, at the point of service) is more cost-effective than responding to complaints after the fact.

The service recovery paradox

The Technical Assistance Research Program (TARP), a program that conducts consumer research for the U.S. Office of Consumer Affairs, discovered what it calls the "service recovery

Service recovery situations

Service failures are inevitable. There is no way that service can be flawless every day of the week, every week of the year. Thus, there are countless opportunities for service recovery, or instances in which a negative experience can be transformed into a positive one. Service recovery situations arise from a variety of factors, including the following:

Mistakes: A patient is brought a liquid meal that was not ordered.

Unrealistic expectations: A patient visiting the ED expects to be seen upon walk-in.

Unexpected circumstances: Patient flow problems creating backups, delays, and waits.

Emergent market demands: Private rooms and inpatient room service are now routinely expected.

Systems breakdown: A formerly well-functioning system breaks down due to some change, such as increased volume, decreased staffing, learning curves for new staff, changes in equipment, or changes in facility design or locations.

Vendor failure: A nursing home does not receive flu vaccinations when expected.

Natural disasters: Hurricanes cause power outages, the need to move patients to other facilities, large influx of patients, and staff shortages.

Compromised patient safety or security: If patients hear about medical errors or past mistakes at your facility, they will automatically be more concerned and apprehensive, which requires greater customer service attention.

paradox," that is, a customer who experienced a problem that is effectively resolved will be more satisfied than a customer who experienced no problems. In fact, TARP research has shown that, across all service industries (including healthcare), customer loyalty can increase up to 8% over loyalty of a customer who experienced no problem.[8]

Indeed, service recovery can be the most important moment in any healthcare encounter. Imagine the possibilities. Every service error is a defining moment for you, your front-line staff, your management, your organization, your reputation, and your brand. The reaction and follow-up demonstrate your organization's real standards and lived values. Service recovery helps transform negative first impressions into positive, lasting memories. Thus, the lasting impression you give your patients is that you represent a caring and thoughtful organization, with their well being first in your thoughts. This has been proven to lead to positive word-of-mouth and employee, physician, and patient loyalty.

ADVERSE EFFECTS OF SERVICE FAILURE WITHOUT RECOVERY

Service failure without recovery, on the other hand, can have significant adverse effects. For example, research shows the following:

- The average company loses about 20% of their customers annually due to poor service.
- Only 4% of unhappy customers complain; the rest simply go away angry.
- For every customer complaint received, there are an average of 24 more people with problems, six of which are severe.
- Of those who complain, 56%–70% will do business with the company again if the complaint is resolved. This percentage increases to 96% if the complaint is resolved quickly.[9]

Effect on corporate customers and health plans

Corporate customers and health plans select providers who satisfy their patients. Pay-for-performance schemes are raising the stakes by adding direct monetary incentives for their members' satisfaction with providers. Health plans do so because they recognize that they must keep their corporate customers and patients satisfied in order to retain their customer base and remain competitive. With changes to how healthcare is provided on the horizon, if individuals are no longer required to move within pre-designated healthcare circles but rather can choose whomever they want, word-of-mouth advertising will become priceless.

WORD-OF-MOUTH

We like to listen to and tell stories. Patients share their experiences, positive or negative, with their family, friends, and acquaintances. Research on several different industries, including healthcare, show that twice as many people will be told about bad experiences than will be told about good experiences:[10]

- The average person who has a complaint tells nine or 10 people about it; 13% tell more than 20 people.
- Customers whose complaints have been resolved tell five to six people.

And in today's technology-driven world, an unresolved complaint is not just shared with the immediate family and neighborhood. It can be broadcast over the Internet via blogs, personal web pages, and e-mail, or on one of the multitude of cable and satellite television stations that provide niche broadcasting.

Marketers in healthcare have long advocated word-of-mouth advertising, not only because it works but also because it costs little or nothing. Investments to increase word-of-mouth communication often have a higher payoff than investments in improving any other service or product in the healthcare system. In fact, it works for healthcare marketing more than for any other industry because the higher price of the product, the greater the likelihood that consumers will complain about its poor performance.[11] Thus, as healthcare costs continue to rise for patients, people will talk more and more.

Emotions run high in healthcare. Making service recovery easy can not only turn a potentially bad experience into a good one, but it also can reduce a patient's urge to tell others about the bad experience. It may even encourage the opposite—the urge to tell others about the positive experience that came out of the negative.

Importance of complaint handling to patients/residents

Press Ganey's 2005 National Healthcare Satisfaction Report found, in a survey of more than two million patients at 1,506 hospitals, that patients ranked response to their complaints or concerns made during their stay as the number one priority item for hospitals to address. Similar surveys of home healthcare patients and residents of assisted living facilities also found the handling of complaints to be one of the top five priority items. Not only is there a strong relationship between handling of complaints and *likelihood of recommending the facility* (which is a predictor of loyalty and word-of-mouth behavior), but there also is a high priority placed on improvement in this area. From the perspective of patients and residents, service recovery may be the most important strategy a healthcare organization can use to achieve service excellence.

EMPLOYEE LOYALTY: EVERYONE'S CONCERN

Employee loyalty is not just a human resources problem; it is a systems issue. High turnover is a sign that something is not right. Organizations with high turnover suffer competitive disadvantage due to higher costs, lost institutional knowledge, and inefficiencies, as it takes time to recruit and train new talent, and workflow is interrupted when temps try to fill in. Not only is such a situation a breeding ground for complaints, it also can create an environment in which complaints may be ignored.

Employee loyalty goes beyond the money saved by not having to train new staff, however. Employees need to feel good about their jobs and the organization if they are to present a good image to patients. When they are happier at work and feeling valued and empowered, loyal employees stay during the hard times. They not only trust that the organization will find a way through but also proactively make contributions vital to its eventual success.

EMPLOYEE EMPOWERMENT

Empowered, loyal employees will take an ownership stake in the organization. They will look for opportunities for savings, efficiency, and innovation. In addition, they will encourage others to work with the organization and help market to their friends and families the benefits of working in just such an organization. All of these benefits improve front-line service delivery.

A primary predictor of employee loyalty and satisfaction—and a crucial component of any successful service recovery program—is employee empowerment. Despite what one might think, our research from surveying thousands of healthcare employees shows that giving employees consideration (i.e., being nice), discretion, and recognition surpass pay and job security as the strongest predictors of employee satisfaction. Empowerment means expanding your trust in everyone you work with by limiting the need to "check with a manager," destroying multiple signature requirements, and encouraging the first person to receive a complaint to see it through to resolution. Employee empowerment is discussed in detail in Chapters 6 and 7.

The more empowered and autonomous employees are, the more likely they are to not only meet but also exceed expectations. Empowered employees reduce customer impatience because they remedy the situation themselves instead of making the customer wait for a

Top five service quality improvement opportunities identified by patients

Acute inpatient facilities

1. Response to concerns/complaints made during your stay
2. Amount of attention paid to your special or personal needs
3. Staff sensitivity to the inconvenience that health problems/hospitalization can cause
4. How well the nurses kept you informed
5. Staff effort to include you in decisions about your treatment

Assisted living facilities

1. Value for your money
2. Responsiveness of management to your ideas
3. Handling of complaints/grievances
4. Extent to which food meets your special diet needs
5. Extent to which management provides a well-run and organized operation

Home health agencies

1. How well home care handled your request to change nurses or aides
2. How well the office dealt with your problems and complaints
3. How well home care handled emergencies
4. Staff's concern to keep your family informed about your treatment, condition, or progress
5. How easy it was to get the visiting schedule changed

Source: Press Ganey Associates National Priority Index for each service, 2004, based on responses received from 2,170,004 patients treated at 1,506 facilities, 2,904 residents at 108 assisted living facilities, and 177,421 home healthcare patients at 404 facilities.

response. Empowering employees to take matters into their own hands also helps them feel that they are valued, trusted members of the organization.

Employees who know what the customer wants and can deliver it often have a feeling of satisfaction that can be transferred to the customer. Employees who want to be empowered, and are, have a higher level of job satisfaction, which leads to increased customer satisfaction. However, be careful with any employees who express discomfort with empowerment. Being forced into empowerment can lead to decreased employee satisfaction and loyalty. This situation is generally rare and easily detectable.

PHYSICIAN LOYALTY

Physicians have a stake in service excellence as much as anyone else. Empowered, satisfied, and loyal staff develop stronger working relationships with physicians and provide a higher level of service to both physicians and their patients. Happy nurses, empowered to handle patient problems quickly and efficiently, will take the same approach to their relationships with physicians.

Physicians want a hospital where they know their patients will receive the highest level of patient care and sincere, dedicated attention from the nursing staff. Physicians will put up with a lot (such as inconveniences and administrative problems) if the quality of care is high.

Other factors that matter to medical staff include the interpersonal skills of nurses and their ability to work with other departments. These employees often bolster the morale of the patients as well, making their recovery easier and swifter, which in turn can ease the physicians' stress and workload. In fact, treatment of patients' service needs has more bearing on physician loyalty than does the treatment of the disease.[12] If patients are taken care of well at a facility, the physician is more likely to maintain his or her relationship with the facility.

Physicians should be involved in service-recovery strategies as well. Today, patients often tell their physicians when things go wrong. Quickly resolving patient care issues strengthens the patient-provider relationship and can prevent lawsuits against both the hospital and the physician. Physicians notice when their patients complain less about the health services they regularly use.

Reducing complaints also reduces the physician's malpractice risk. Knowledge that their patient will be treated well, that health service providers always do absolutely anything and everything to resolve patient complaints, and that their own complaints as a physician will be taken seriously, all encourage positive physician relations. Overall, strong service recovery programs improve the retention and recruitment of valuable medical talent.

MONEY TALKS: FOUR HOSPITAL SUCCESS STORIES

The bottom line is that service recovery works. It has worked for our healthcare partners, and it will continue to work in the future as consumers become more knowledgeable, informed, and empowered to choose their healthcare providers.

A good service recovery program will affect a facility's profit margin. Empowered employees will be loyal and happy, which will reduce staff turnover and reduce the amount of money spent on new employee training. Positive employee word-of-mouth will build your brand reputation, attract more patients, and draw talent. Word-of-mouth is not only free advertising and recruiting, but it's also the most powerful. People trust what they hear from friends and family more than any other message or advertisement. Improved patient satisfaction means process improvement, a rise in productivity, and a decrease in costs. It also will affect marketability when the revenues go up as the positive word-of-mouth spreads.

Conemaugh Memorial Medical Center (Johnstown, PA)

Conemaugh Memorial Medical Center was losing $2 million a month from operations, had Press Ganey inpatient percentile ranks of less than 22%, and was losing market share. Reengineering and business process redesign initiatives didn't work.

Leadership challenged everyone to focus on more than the financial issues. The top three priorities for all decision-making became clinical excellence, service excellence, and cost effectiveness. Conemaugh's Service Excellence Initiative included teams charged with inpatient and outpatient satisfaction, employee satisfaction, physician satisfaction, service recovery, measurement, facility improvements, leadership development, and performance standards.

> As a result of these programs, patient satisfaction soared from the 22nd percentile to the 93rd percentile, and admissions increased by 6% in one year. The $2 million a month average loss turned into an average gain of $370,000 a month.

St. Vincent's Hospital (Birmingham, AL)

St. Vincent's was facing increasingly aggressive competition from the more than 10 hospitals in their area and experienced poor financial performance for the year. It needed to leverage its reputation for quality and high-tech care into increased market share and enhanced financial performance. St. Vincent's service excellence initiative was designed to refocus on its core values and mission, which call for extraordinary service as a "healing ministry of Jesus Christ." The foundation of the service excellence effort was accurate, timely, and actionable measurement and data. All Press Ganey reports are posted to the intranet for all employees to review. The first report placed them in the 58th percentile.

The hospital did the following:

- Developed a far-reaching education plan and integrated expectations and standards into orientation.
- Developed leadership expectations for management.
- Created rewards/recognition programs.
- *Created a service recovery program.* The program was designed to capture input from associates, managers, patients, and visitors and empowered associates to "make it right."
- Used unique and creative communications (e.g., departmental service excellence bulletin boards, skits, video presentations, music, flyers on standards, service excellence site on the intranet, fun activities).
- Hosted celebrations.
- Had guest speakers and special presentations to re-energize associates.
- Interwove service excellence throughout other initiatives, such as process improvement initiatives. Press Ganey results are a standing agenda item at all management and departmental meetings.

In the span of nine months, St. Vincent's went from the 58th percentile of all hospitals in the Press Ganey database to the 89th percentile and achieved its goal of reaching the 91st percentile one year later. Their peer-group (300–449 bed groups) percentile rank was 96th. They experienced "significantly improved revenue." Inpatient discharges increased by 8% and outpatient visits are up 12% over the previous year.

Somerset Medical Center (Somerville, NJ)

Somerset Medical Center was sailing into its second century of service when it hit an iceberg—the results of its first Press Ganey survey. Scores for the first quarter of 2000 ranked the medical center in the 58th percentile for emergency department (ED) satisfaction, in the 39th percentile for outpatient satisfaction, in the 35th percentile for inpatient satisfaction, and in the 22nd percentile for ambulatory satisfaction.

Somerset Medical Center's new CEO charged the medical center's Senior Vice President of Patient Care with the task of identifying problem areas and implementing strategies to improve patient satisfaction. A steering committee of key managers and staff was formed. The next step was to recruit other staff members to form subcommittees.

Over the past three years, Somerset Medical Center has implemented a wide range of programs to improve patient satisfaction, including the following:

- Secret shoppers who interview patients and staff to see how well employees are exhibiting recommended standards of behavior.
- Thank you cards for all inpatients.
- *A service recovery program.*
- A mandatory three-hour customer service orientation program for all new employees and ongoing customer service education thereafter.
- Quarterly reward and recognition programs honoring employees.
- A monthly honor roll distributed to each department.
- Monetary incentives to department managers for meeting goals in patient satisfaction scores.

In 2002, the medical center reached the 99th percentile in ED and inpatient satisfaction in the fourth quarter. Outpatient satisfaction soared to the 95th percentile, and ambulatory satisfaction topped the 92nd percentile for the fourth quarter of 2002.

These results have translated into an improved bottom line: The medical center has noted dramatic growth in patient volume in virtually all clinical departments and has experienced a 51% increase in net patient revenue over the past three years. The medical center boasts an astounding 4.5% nursing vacancy rate, which is well below the state average of 18%.

Cancer Treatment Centers of America (Tulsa, OK)

Cancer Treatment Centers of America has consistently scored in the upper 99th percentile of hospitals in Press Ganey's patient satisfaction database. In 2000, the hospital won a Press Ganey Compass Award for being one of the most improved clients in the database. Before initiating its patient satisfaction program, the hospital experienced a $6.4 million loss. Within ten years of establishing the program, the hospital reported a $15.2 million profit. Patient retention and revenue were up, as was patient satisfaction. In 1990, 100% of Cancer

Treatment Centers of America's patients came from advertising. Today, between 40% and 60% of all new patients come from patient referrals and word-of-mouth.

Is your organization ready?

Is your organization ready to allow staff the power to do whatever it takes, bending the rules a little, to meet customer needs? To be ready for empowerment also means having both cultural support and leadership support. Cultivate a culture of service excellence by defining service standards, promoting standards, assessing adherence to standards, adjusting standards to changing needs and expectations, recognizing service recovery opportunities, and always, always, always having leaders and managers model excellent service behaviors.

Before diving in, assess your organization, its leadership, and its culture to determine the level of organizational readiness for an organization-wide service recovery and empowerment initiative. Do so formally through organizational culture surveys/focus groups, informally by talking to people individually and in groups, or by circulating the Organizational Readiness quiz on the CD that accompanies this book.

Endnotes

1. National Performance Review, *Serving the American Public: Best Practices in Resolving Customer Complaints. Federal Benchmarking Consortium Study Report* (Washington, DC: U.S. Government Printing Office, November 6, 1996).

2. Ron Zemke and Chip R. Bell, *Knock Your Socks Off Service Recovery* (New York: AMACOM, 2000): 8.

3. Betsy Gelb and Madeline Johnson, "Word-of-mouth communication: Causes and consequences," *Journal of Health Care Marketing* 15, no. 3 (Fall 1995): 54–8.

4. Leonard L. Berry and Jonathan A. Leighton, "Restoring Customer Confidence." *Medical Health Services* (Spring 2004): 17.

5. Janelle Barlow and Claus Moller, *A Complaint is a Gift.* (Berrett-Koehler, Inc., 1996).

6. Maxwell Drain and Dennis Kaldenberg, "Building Patient Loyalty and Trust: The role of patient satisfaction," *Group Practice Journal* (October 1999): 32.

7. Richard S. Lytle, Peter W. Hom, and Michael P. Mokwa, "Serv*Or: An Organizational Measure of Service Orientation," *Journal of Retailing* 74, no. 4 (1998): 462.

8. Consumer Complaint Handling in America: An Update Study, Part I (TARP: September 30, 1985).

9. Bonnie Jameson and Betsy Sanders, Fabled Service: *Ordinary acts, extraordinary outcomes.* (San Francisco: Jossey-Bass, 1995).

10. John Goodman (TARP), "Basic Facts on Customer Complaint Behavior and the Impact of Service on the Bottom Line," *Competitive Advantage* (June 1999): 1–5.

11. Gelb and Johnson, *supra* note 3.

12. Liz Osborne, *Resolving Patient Complaints: A Step-by-Step Guide to Effective Service Recovery* (Boston: Jones and Bartlett Publishers, Inc., 2004).

CHAPTER 5

CULTURE:
GETTING EVERYONE TO WALK THE PATH TO SERVICE EXCELLENCE

Authors: Kelly Nemeth, Randall S. Blum,
Julie Tittle-Plank, Aris Relias-Clark

Any program you create must be in tune with your organizational goals, mission, and culture. If your current mission does not recognize the importance of service excellence, let alone recovery, any program you create may be doomed to fail. Service recovery needs to be ingrained into staff behavior—it must be part of their daily routine and organizational culture.

How you create your service-recovery program can both move (or improve) your organizational culture toward service excellence and increase employee and medical staff buy-in for the idea of service recovery as an organizational and personal approach to daily behavior.

Employee buy-in plays a significant role in the success of the program because everything depends upon front-line staff engaging in service-recovery behaviors. Instead of dictating to staff what they must do, collaborate with them, and together you can determine what service-recovery practices and system will be most successful. You as a leader will bring lots of ideas to the table, and so will they. You'll know what worked well at other facilities (from, among other things, reading this book), but they will have a better sense of what would work best for their departments and teams—just because something worked well elsewhere does not mean that it will work for you.

There are no shortcuts; you must work together. And remember, change is often difficult. Make sure that you create a process to which staff will be highly receptive.

Even if your current culture is service oriented, there is still opportunity to become world class. If you find yourself in this position, strive for phenomenal! Furthermore, as healthcare

Tips for improving culture

Smile. A smile is one of the first things people notice. Smiles send a positive message and are also contagious. Consider putting a mirror in front of people who answer the phone to remind them to smile.

Treat each other well. Smile at each other and treat associates, colleagues, supervisors, and everyone else with whom you work with respect, dignity, understanding, patience, and love. This behavior sets a tone that will flow into interactions with patients and family.

Greet each other. Many people walk around as if it is a faux pas to look someone in the eye and say hello. Greeting others is a step in the right direction to improving culture. Whenever possible, take a minute to introduce yourself, and let associates introduce themselves.

Recognize employees. When you catch someone in the act of doing something well, recognize them for it then and there. Encourage senior management to do so too.

Make sure that staff are supported and that they know that they are supported. Talk with them to find out what is working well and where there are opportunities for improvement. Experience has shown that the only departments that use the service recovery program consistently are those with true management support.

Survey employees. Find out where the gaps lie and where your strengths are. Work on your weaknesses, and build on your strengths. As you make improvements, make them visible so that staff know that their thoughts are important.

Hold everyone accountable. Make sure that everyone from the top down "walks the walk and talks the talk." Tie expectations into everyone's performance reviews and incentive programs. Some organizations set aside a per-person service recovery budget (that is, how much that individual staff member can authorize in terms of free coupons, etc., to make something right) and hold staff accountable for spending their budget.

becomes increasingly competitive, everyone is working constantly to improve—anyone standing on these tracks will be run over. There are always going to be areas that you can improve.

Leadership support: What's important gets talked about and done

Where is your organization's focus? A service-oriented culture has a pervasive focus on serving both internal and external customers.

A culture of service excellence begins with talking about the service you provide currently and envisioning a future higher level of service. Make service excellence an agenda item at all meetings. Consider the implications of your policies, procedures, and management decisions on customer service. Never stop asking what you and your team or department can do to serve customers better. Cultures of service excellence are typified by people relentlessly working to make service excellent and by a pervasive belief that only excellent service behavior is acceptable.

Likewise, praise the best people—those who typify either great service or the "steady-consistent" providers of solid, good service. Tell stories about those on your team and on other teams who deliver great service or do the little things that make healthcare happen. Tell stories about the potential for great service. Make your vision of a service excellence future come alive by talking about it.

MAKE YOUR ACTIONS REFLECT YOUR VALUES

Leadership support can also be shown through the actions that are taken after complaints are received. Read all comments received from customer surveys and your complaint-tracking mechanism. Assign complaints or problems to the leader responsible for that area. That person should resolve the issue within a specified period of time. Publicly report on a regular basis the status of these dozens of ongoing complaint resolutions. This type of action demonstrates that leaders are serious about listening to the voice of the customer. In addition, when employees see leadership dedicated to improvement based on complaints, they will be encouraged to continue gathering feedback and reporting it. Such leadership practices also have been shown to improve employee satisfaction and loyalty.

CULTURE INFLUENCES BEHAVIOR

At the Four Seasons Hotel, Vice President John Sharpe recognizes that the customer isn't always right but that staff should always err in favor of the customer. His oft-repeated mantra is, "No one will ever criticize a staffer for making a guest happy." Because of this attitude and the fact that the message has been clearly passed down to line managers, this expectation has become so culturally embedded that staff check each other if anyone says anything negative about someone or does something strange, weird, or above-and-beyond for the customer.

When leadership truly backs employees, the effect always shines through in these interactions. This support can be shown in various ways. For example, recognize employees who exceed standards and epitomize service culture. Eliminate punishment for reporting complaints; instead, reward service recovery opportunity identification and action.

WHAT IS ENCOURAGED? WHAT IS DISCOURAGED?

Good managers exert a strong influence over their teams, which is part of what makes them good. What behaviors are unacceptable? What behaviors do they encourage and reward? What do they discourage or frown upon?

If a wrong behavior goes unchecked, it shows employees and patients that it is permissible. In addition, think carefully about what behaviors are rewarded in your culture. Who receives management attention? Is it those who provide outstanding service, or is it the squeaky wheels? Who receives public rewards or even the little benefits, such as time off when they need it?

Determine what behaviors you want to see individuals on your staff display. To encourage these behaviors most effectively, create a schedule to positively reinforce them at least once a week. Always carry around gifts, cafeteria gift cards, candy, or at least a heartfelt "thank you" so you are prepared to offer positive reinforcement and recognition on the spot. This takes a different approach and a degree of discipline, but if you maintain it consistently for three to six months, you'll see a change in culture.

The Centegra Health System experience

Changing culture across an entire organization or service line sometimes takes a tremendous force or wake-up call.

Mike Eesley, CEO of Centegra Health System (a Press Ganey Success Story Winner[1]) had a self-described life-changing experience after he broke his hip in two places, tore up his knee, and spent more than a year in rehab. During that time, he felt like a helpless captive, forced to rely on others to care for his needs. He summed up his experience in one line: "Great hospital, great surgeon, but the experience was ruined by a nurse named Ben."

During Eesley's immediate period of recuperation, a jumble of thoughts and emotions cycled through his mind. "Will I recover? How can I provide for my family? Will I have a job? Can I ever play with my children again?" During this time, Ben would walk into Eesley's room and complain profusely about his own life, his wife, and so on—completely ignoring Eesley's emotional and physical state. Over the weeks of recuperation, Ben never stopped complaining, and after a while, the family found Ben's behavior so disruptive that they would call before visiting to make sure Ben was not there.

Of the estimated 52 different people with whom a patient interacts during the day, it only takes one to make the stay miserable. There must be consistency and reliability in service across the entire organization. The organizational culture must be singularly focused on service excellence.

EESLEY'S 12 RECOMMENDATIONS TO INSTILL A CULTURE OF CUSTOMER SERVICE

To make broad changes to an organization's culture in a short period of time requires serious horsepower. Eesley recommends 12 actions to create a culture of customer service:

1. Take a time-out to discern and create your strategy.

2. Act on top leaders who are out of alignment with the customer service approach.

3. Invite board members to join you in visibility strategies.

4. Embrace and master the art of storytelling. One of the most effective means of spreading new ideas is through stories, so identify your passionate stories and master the art of sharing them.

5. Create multiple visibility strategies (e.g., round-the-clock open forums, general orientation, rounds, CEO newsletter).

6. The work of healthcare is the work of the heart. Therefore, champion emotional intelligence.

7. Reward and recognize until you are tired of doing so, and then do more.

8. Stay focused on the message of customer satisfaction.

9. Fund leadership development and lifelong learning for all. Read books and facilitate dialogue on what is learned.

10. Declare a servant-leadership model of leadership (that is, where the leaders also serve those they lead), and hold leaders accountable for moving beyond management to transformational servant-leadership.

11. Accept the fact that large-scale transformation can only evolve when lots of people at all levels of your healthcare organization start to do things differently.

12. Recognize that people must act with awareness that we are all interdependent in a healthcare organization. Get everyone engaged in the process of service.

Measure employee and physician satisfaction

A culture of service excellence is not just about the patient-customers; it's also about your employees and physicians. High performers in patient satisfaction value the contributions of employees and medical staff by putting them on the same pedestals as patient-customers in terms of their right to respect, dignity, and excellent customer service.

The healthcare world is heavily interconnected between patients, employees, and physicians. Therefore, it is not surprising that their respective evaluations of the same experience tend to be similar. High patient satisfaction has been shown to be the result of high employee and medical staff satisfaction, and a service-oriented culture will apply all the tools and techniques of customer service excellence, including service recovery, to all customers including their fellow employees and medical staff. Ask anyone—this attitude and approach consistently creates a more positive, enjoyable atmosphere or culture.

To create this atmosphere at your organization, first measure the satisfaction of employees and medical staff. Asking associates or physicians to improve their service to patients carries a lot more credence when you demonstrate a willingness to ask your own staff for their perspectives and then act upon the data to improve their experience at your facility. Going the extra mile for an associate models the service excellence behavior and attitude, encouraging the associate to go the extra mile for the customer—indeed, employees will treat customers only as well as they themselves are treated.

Case study: How one hospital did it

Robert Wood Johnson University Hospital is a not-for-profit 200-bed acute care community hospital in Hamilton, NJ. Its mission is "Excellence through Service" and it guides its actions based on five values: quality, understanding, excellence, service, and teamwork.

According to Deborah Cardello, RN, MSN, CHE, Chief Operating Officer, the hospital began to use Press Ganey in 1998 to benchmark patient satisfaction, and for the first quarter of 1999, it was in the 44th percentile. That ranking challenged the hospital to drive change aggressively. With a committed senior leadership and a focus on employees, the organization has created a culture of service excellence using innovative approaches that have resulted in increased employee and patient satisfaction.

PATIENT SATISFACTION

Many program elements that the hospital adopted were traditional and grounded in research and practice. For example, directors round daily and identify issues before they become problems. Staff members receive feedback based on patterns and trends identified by the director. An active approach to improving systems and processes is used. All staff members are invited to use a line of credit from the gift shop and apologize to patients whom we have disappointed.

Other patient satisfaction initiatives and programs include the following:

- Service representatives and greeters are located in key areas throughout the facility. They work with families to give information, refreshments, other amenities, and support as needed. They carry the service hotline phone, a number that patients or family may call to bring an issue to the hospital's attention. Signs with the hotline number are posted in patient rooms, as well as in reception areas. Beepers are distributed to families waiting for updates so they may visit the gift shop or cafeteria and not miss the doctor.

- The "Art and Soul" program promotes the wellbeing of our patients and employees. Volunteers provide an array of services, including complimentary therapy, pet therapy, prescription for laughter, soothing bedside music, and intergenerational art activities.

- A member of the food and nutrition department delivers complimentary fruit baskets to each new admission. This visit also serves as an introduction to the food services staff and familiarizes patients with the food selection and distribution process.

- A supportive care coordinator position was developed in 2001 to lead the organizational efforts in improving pain management. The coordinator serves as an educator and consultant and, more importantly, functions as a change agent and patient rights advocate.

- "Loving Spoonfuls" is a program to provide opportunities for our non-patient care staff to interact with patients. They report to nursing units, help pass out patient trays, assist with feeding, and talk to patients. Participating staff members feel connected to the mission.

EMPLOYEE SATISFACTION

Cardello believes that there is a strong correlation between patient and employee satisfaction. One of most effective ways management keeps in touch with our employees is through its Employee Satisfaction Committee. Examples of changes made based on employee feedback include increases in tuition reimbursement, improved vacation policy, healthier food in the cafeteria, and the development of an employee fitness program.

The hospital's fourth-quarter employee satisfaction results reflect improvement in 11 of 15 subscales. Its overall composite employee satisfaction scores increased from the 67th to the 87th percentile. Most impressive were our results in customer focus subscale (97th percentile), satisfaction with senior leadership (98th percentile), and recognition subscale (91st percentile).

RESULTS

According to Cardello, Robert Wood Johnson Hospital was the fastest-growing hospital in the state for three years in a row, with an unprecedented growth in the number of inpatient, emergency department, and operating room admissions since 1999, and one of two hospitals to ever win the Gold Level NJ Governor's Award. A new three-story building was constructed based on this growth, and a new cancer center was targeted for fall 2002. She notes that the hospital enjoys a secure financial position and increases in market share, as well as a declining length of stay. The hospital attributes its success to the commitment of senior leaders and to the evolvement of a culture focused on employee and patient satisfaction.

Endnote

1. This success story, and all other Press Ganey Success Story winners can be accessed at *www.pressganey.com/client_recognition/success_stories/default.php.*

CHAPTER 6

TEN ORGANIZATION BUILDING BLOCKS FOR A SUCCESSFUL SERVICE RECOVERY PROGRAM

Authors: Kelly Nemeth, Randall S. Blum, Julie Tittle-Plank, Aris Relias-Clark

Many people enter into the healthcare system with the assumption that the experience is not going to be pleasant. Healthcare services fall into a category known as "negative" services—that is, most people go to a physician or hospital only when there is a problem (e.g., they are sick or need an unpleasant diagnostic procedure). It's like going to the dentist or the car repair shop: Few people look forward to it, and the popular media tends to cover the negative stories more than the positive ones."[1]

You must counteract the natural assumption that a healthcare experience will be bad with the idea that it can be a very positive experience. The best way to do so is to create a program that allows you to reply to concerns and complaints in a fair and effective manner while at the same time tracking those complaints to avoid future problems with the same issue. Quick recovery bolsters the returns of a service recovery program. Immediate reaction to a problem tells patients that their concerns are a top priority for the organization and conveys respect and concern.

What are the elements that your organization must have in place in order to implement a successful service recovery program?

To create such a successful service recovery program you must have at least ten building blocks:

1. Understanding, meeting, and exceeding customer expectations
2. Effective communication
3. Awareness
4. Leadership
5. Empowerment
6. Accountability
7. Reliability
8. Teamwork
9. Attitude
10. Recognition

Block 1: Understanding customer expectations

The gap between customer expectations for a particular service and how that service is actually delivered defines how satisfied a customer will be. Expectations exist for reliability, responsiveness, tangibles, assurance, and empathy. Similarly, when a service recovery opportunity arises, customers have certain expectations of how it should be resolved. Customers typically use three criteria[2] to judge how an organization responds to their complaints:

- The treatment they receive when lodging the complaint
- The response to the complaint (with particular emphasis on speed)
- The outcome of the complaint, such as an apology or compensation

'SHOULD' VS. 'WILL' EXPECTATIONS

In all exchanges, people have expectations about what should happen and what will happen during an encounter. These expectations are shaped by previous experience, word-of-mouth communications, and the service provider's communications. These expectations provide the basis for comparison against which performance is measured, which, in turn, affects perceptions of service quality.[3]

A "will expectation" is what customers believe will actually happen during a service encounter. "Should expectations" are based on a normative standard of what ought to happen.[4]

Will expectations

Research in the healthcare industry has found that, in terms of will expectations, 55% of the respondents believed complaints would be ignored. Worse yet, only 8% expected an apology to be made and only 5% thought the staff member would empathize. Furthermore, only 28% thought that staff would explain the service that was provided, and only 17% thought that staff would be responsive to their complaint.[5]

Should expectations

The research on should expectations found that the number one "should" was to explain the service provided (46%), followed by "responsiveness" (42%), other (20%), an apology (16%), policy change (15%), and empathy (11%). It seems that much of what patients want in the event of a healthcare service failure is education, information, and a sense that the person taking their complaint is actually going to do something about it.

Consumer service recovery expectations

People differ in their requirements for being fully satisfied with a service-recovery experience. For some, an apology is enough even for the greatest of offenses, whereas others make big demands for miniscule mishaps.

Researchers have found that socio-cultural backgrounds account for these differences.[6] They identified three frameworks that ground consumer expectation:

- Consumer motivated by a desire to maintain a positive, *personal* relationship with the provider and institution simply seek an apology or a sense of reconciliation.
- Consumers under an *individualism/control* influence find themselves at the "center of the universe" and desire to be placed on a pedestal or treated with reverence. In this highly emotional framework, the consumer wants to feel important and to co-design (or, even, personally select) the solution.
- Consumers with a *utilitarian perspective* consider service recovery a success when they have been adequately compensated for the time, money, and value lost. This can be completely devoid of emotions.

Recognizing that there are different frameworks means that a one-size-fits-all solution will not work. The service-recovery approach used by staff should include the ability to adjust responses to concerns/complaints to fit these different expectations.

IMPROVE STAFF RESPONSIVENESS

Responsiveness refers to a patient's belief that the person taking the complaint can and will do something to help and show they care. This is where service recovery comes into play. Research has shown that customers will give you only two chances to get it right. They won't give you a third chance. On the other hand, research also shows that people do not expect perfect service at all times. Therefore, it is not the actual service failure that affects customer satisfaction, but it is the actions—that is, recovery—following the failure or poor service that results in (dis)satisfaction.

MAKE ASKING QUESTIONS ABOUT EXPECTATIONS A STANDARD PART OF SERVICE DELIVERY

To exceed expectations, you need to know what they are. Should expectations are often unique and individualized for patients and families. To ensure that you get it right the first time, integrate questions that solicit customer expectations into the actual service delivery. The chances are very good that your customer will be reasonable. Simply asking customers what they expect and then either fulfilling or adjusting the expectation accordingly is clearly a best practice.

> **THREE RULES TO SERVICE RECOVERY:**
>
> - *Do it right the first time*
> - *Fix it properly if it ever fails*
> - *There are no third chances*
>
> —Leonard Berry, PhD,
> Texas A&M University

Block 2: Effective communication

In order to understand and act on customer needs, frontline staff must be able to communicate with customers. Effective communication entails verbal and nonverbal communication, telephone etiquette, active listening skills, and demonstrating to customers that what they have to say is important to you. These skills can be taught and must be practiced.

Verbal and nonverbal communication

Empathy and understanding are the two most important aspects of communication in service recovery. Although, ideally, all staff would already know how to do so, it usually takes significant training and practice to achieve consistent empathetic communication delivery. The objective is to have a staff that can respond to patients and family on an emotional level and remain aware of the emotional component of care in their daily practice.

> *"Inferior care results when health professionals lack full mastery of their clinical areas or cannot communicate effectively and compassionately."*
>
> —Kathleen N. Lohr[7]

Nurses typically benefit the most from this training, as they interact with patients frequently and are almost always present. When nurses are truly empathetic, patients' emotional distress is significantly reduced. Patients are also more likely to disclose concerns and questions that can help nurses and physicians to identify other possible clinical problems, such as infections or misunderstanding about self-care, etc. Unfortunately, studies find that empathetic behaviors are rare in most nursing practice. Workshops can be used to help improve the skills of clinicians—the use of role-playing and simulated patients is especially useful for practicing customer service or empathetic communication skills.

Empathetic communication follows a simple formula:

- *Perception* of a verbal or nonverbal cue from the patient that indicates an aspect of his or her emotional experience.
- *Identification* and internal understanding of the emotion present in the patient.
- *Feedback, action, or communication* to the patient to appropriately indicate empathy for the patient's emotion, situation, etc.

There are six practices that can help facilitate communication. These practices, which pay specific attention to perceiving and identifying with the patient's emotional experience, are set forth below.[8]

1. Active listening—Includes eye contact, position, posture, mirrored facial expression, and facilitative responses (e.g., *hmm . . . uh-huh*).

2. Framing or sign posting—Action used to initiate an empathetic response when certainty is lacking.

Let's see if I have this right . . .
It sounds like what you're telling me is . . .
Sounds like . . .

3. Reflecting the content—Mirrors the factual content of patient's statement with similar "nature and intensity."

So you were fine until this morning when you woke up with pain in your belly, and it's been growing more severe ever since.

Sounds like you think that you have appendicitis and that you might need to go into the hospital.

So, if I'm hearing you right, what you really enjoy is going out at night with your friends and having a few drinks.

4. Identify and calibrate the emotion—Response to potent feelings where emotional content is certain but precise character is questionable.

Tell me how you're feeling about this.

I have the sense that you feel strongly, but I'm not sure I understand exactly what the feeling is. Can you tell me?

I can imagine that this might feel . . .

5. Responding to emotions—Use words such as bother, annoy, upset, and uneasy.

Sadness: *That must have been a pretty painful experience for you; you sound like it was very sad.*

Fear: *Sounds like you were really frightened when you discovered that lump.*

Anger: *That situation really got to you, didn't it? I can imagine how angry I'd feel if that happened to me.*

Distrust: *It seems you're not sure whether you should trust me further after I didn't get that test result back to you last week.*

Ambivalence: *It seems to me that you're caught in a bind about whether to stop smoking.*

6. Request and accept corrections—*Did I miss anything? Anything I left out?*
Often, a pause or waiting a significant period of time to respond will be helpful and effective.

Telephone etiquette

The best healthcare organizations define and enforce standards for telephone etiquette. Often, the lack of a customer's direct presence leads us to treat them unconsciously with less priority and attention than those we see. These standards clarify the expectations for minimal service, create consistency in service delivery, and encourage customer-friendly behavior:

- Everyone should know how to operate the telephones in their areas, including how to put a caller on hold and how to transfer a call.
- Calls must be answered within X rings (most organizations state three rings).
- A smile on your face reflects in your tone of voice.
- Answer calls with your name, title, and department, asking, "How may I help you?" or a similar greeting.
- Speak clearly; Use a tone of voice that is alert, pleasant, natural, and expressive.
- Don't yell or talk to others while on the phone.
- When transferring a call, provide the direct number in case the call is lost.
- Put a caller on hold when looking for someone within your area to assist him or her.
- Ask permission before putting the caller on hold. Upon return, thank the caller for holding.
- Return all calls (and e-mails) promptly, within a standard time frame. Most organizations use 24 hours.
- Do not chew gum, suck on candy, eat, or drink while on the phone.
- Provide assistance to callers who have incorrectly reached your phone. Transfer them to the appropriate person/department, and offer them a direct phone number prior to transfer in case they need to call again.

Handling complaints over the phone requires a different technique and style than handling them in person. Listening is more difficult. Expressing empathy and confirming understanding of the concern is difficult when you can't show or see facial expressions and reactions. Frequent practice is critical to building these skills.

Finally, make sure staff understand the types of telephone call related demands customers have. For example, have the answers to commonly asked questions printed up and distributed or posted near the phone. A popular tactic among intensive care units is to establish a single person as the contact for all of a patient's friends and family. Instead of receiving four or more calls per day per patient, the nurse makes a regularly scheduled call to one of the patient's primary caregivers.

Active listening skills

Active listening, itself, sometimes can calm and satisfy the concerned party. Active listening is a critical skill that can be taught and learned. It involves a range of behaviors, such as listening without interrupting, nodding the head, making gestures, expressing acknowledgement and concern, reflecting the content, gauging emotions, avoiding destructive nonverbal behaviors (e.g., annoyed looks, standing by the door, doing other things, lack of eye contact, etc.), and not making assumptions about the person or situation.

Individuals voice complaints differently. Some will be irate, others passive, others will be aggressive, still others will indicate the seriousness of their complaint by the tenor of their voice. Similarly, as noted earlier, individual patients will have different preferences for a service recovery. Some will only be satisfied with a gift or other form of compensation, while others will be ecstatic with an apology.

Because what people want in terms of service recovery depends upon largely individual sociocultural backgrounds, active listening is required before you can act. Understand fully what the person expects to be done before you rush off to do something. Some examples of positive, empathetic responses for active listening include the following:

- You seem upset. Please tell me more.
- Perhaps I've misunderstood. Can you please explain that to me again?
- I'm glad you brought this to my attention. I'd like to look into it.
- If I understand correctly, you're saying that . . .
- I can appreciate how you're feeling about this.
- I can see how upsetting this is to you.
- It certainly sounds as though we've caused you some inconvenience.
- I know I'd be upset, too, if that happened to me.

The nonverbal response is an equally important aspect of active listening. Active listeners should do the following:

- Keep calm.
- Keep the focus on the customer.
- Respect privacy.
- Learn the power of being quiet.
- Use affective body language and cues.
- Write down vital information.

Verbal barriers to active listening

Starting any sentence with, "Yes, but . . . ," is a major barrier to active listening.

Similarly, a response that babbles on and on is a sure sign that someone is not really actively listening. For example, the following response starts off fine, but it soon gets lost in unnecessary and irrelevant detail—"I'm sorry. We're really busy today, you know several staff members are out sick, and we were understaffed to begin with because it's a holiday . . . plus we've had several emergencies . . ."

Demonstrate to customers that what they say is important to you

Finally, do not forget to show patients that they are important through word and deed. It can be hard to do this with a highly charged, emotional customer. Someone spewing anger, sadness, helplessness, or irrationality can evoke emotions in us. Therefore, train staff to not get caught in the emotion of the moment; instead, focus on the customer's needs. When dealing with an emotional customer, follow these four steps, adopted from the Beebe Medical Center.

1. Develop self-awareness

- Assess your own emotional state: Are you mad, anxious, stressed, defensive?
- Assess how this customer or the problem is affecting you: Are you biased?
- Determine whether you have any preconceptions, biases, or other reactions that are getting in the way of communicating with your customers.
- Watch your body language; maintain a neutral stance.
- Are you breathing quickly? Breathe slowly and deeply to relax yourself.
- Allow the customer to vent.
- Focus on the problem, not on the customer's behavior.
- Do not take the customer's comments personally.

2. Employ active listening

- Avoid interrupting; no matter how heated someone gets, they will eventually stop talking.
- Stop doing everything else and focus on your customer.
- Listen carefully to what the customer is saying.
- Validate emotions with affirmations, such as "You're right, it shouldn't have been that difficult."
- Label the customer's feelings. Repeat or paraphrase what the customer says.
- Ask if what you repeated is correct. Apologize.

3. Ask questions and analyze the situation

- Many problems occur because employees do not know the full story, so even if you think you know the full story, allow the customer to tell you.
- Ask for permission to ask questions and then ask questions that verify and clarify in an organized sequence. First verify that you understand fully.
- Ask open-ended questions that require more than a yes or no answer.
- If necessary, contact others for information.

4. Work with the customer to develop an action plan

- Clearly communicate policies/procedures and other constraints.
- Present possible solutions and help the customer understand the benefits/consequences.
- Ask the customer what alternative appeals to him or her the most. If none of the alternatives appeal, solicit customer input.
- Once a solution has been agreed on, state positively and specifically what will be done and when this action will take place.
- Always follow through with action, later in their stay, or after their stay with a phone call.
- Give the customer your name and number; ask the customer to contact you if a problem occurs and they need help in the future.
- Develop standard solutions to common problems in your area.

Implement core service behavior standards

When trying to influence hundreds or thousands of people, the standards for behavior need to be clear and unequivocal. Potential employees and medical staff need to know the standards and agree to them before even completing an application. Leaders must model behavior and reinforce it through training and communication. Appendix E provides examples of standards used by healthcare organizations recognized as high-performers or top-improvers. Standards are also included in the CD that accompanies this book.

If you already have standards and they don't seem to work, remember that there is a difference between a policy on paper and actual behaviors. For example, if despite your policy, less than 80% of the staff actually say, "Is there anything else I can do for you?" every time they leave a patient's room your policy is only worth the paper it's printed on.

Gather teams of front-line staff members across multiple disciplines to develop a set of specific behaviors tied directly into your organization's mission, vision, and values. Making behavior standards tangible is a way of measuring yourselves to assess if you are living the values. Standards should be universally applicable. Some organizations put together booklets explaining the meaning of standards to augment training. Examples of some of these booklets are contained in the CD that accompanies this book.

Examples of standard communications

Anyone who leaves a patient room should say, "Is there anything else I can do or get for you? I have time."

Anyone responding to a delay should say, "Please accept my apology for the delay; I know your time is important and we are doing everything we can to get to you in about __ minutes. Can I get you a blanket, drink, magazine, etc.?"

Before providing care or treatment, say, "I am concerned about your privacy, so I am closing this curtain/door."

Anyone observing someone who appears to be lost should say, "May I take you where you are going?"

Block 3: Awareness

Awareness may be the most overlooked building block to an effective service recovery program. Your organization must become aware on two levels. First, every employee must be aware of service recovery and other service excellence strategies. Second, your leaders and managers must become aware of the exact problems that customers are experiencing in service breakdowns—and how to resolve them on a systems-level.

EMPLOYEE AWARENESS OF THE SERVICE-RECOVERY PROGRAM AND OTHER SERVICE-EXCELLENCE STRATEGIES

Anybody can build a service-recovery program, but building awareness strong enough to change individual behavior is difficult. People must connect their actions to the fact that patients are evaluating those actions—often on a survey within a week of their stay. Everyone is so caught up in the daily grind that managers must make a dedicated effort to communicate the facts about patient satisfaction to all staff. Ask yourself these questions:

- Have *all* staff been shown the patient satisfaction survey?
- Does everyone understand the survey process?
- Have you shared the results? Have all staff seen your scores and how you compare to the nation at large and other facilities like you?
- Do staff know the implications of the scores? Low scores mean that patients and families won't be coming back.
- Do staff hear the negative *and positive* comments that patients write on their surveys about the care they received?
- Do staff understand the level of importance your leaders and managers place on excellence in customer service?
- Do physicians know all of this information?

AWARENESS OF CUSTOMER EXPERIENCES IN SERVICE BREAKDOWNS

An investigation of service breakdowns must begin with knowledge of exactly how your patients and family members experience them. What is prompting the most vocal complaints and most unpleasant concerns? What about these particular situations triggers negative reactions from your patients and family members?

> *"Service breakdowns often attract more attention than 'seamless,' flawless delivery."*
>
> —Len Berry[9]

Do you know what people in the community are actually saying about your hospital? What is the first thing former patients say when asked by friends about their stay? You can't just rely on formal complaints to uncover problems, because most dissatisfied people don't make formal complaints. You need an ongoing commitment to seek out the truth by amassing feedback from numerous listening posts. Although several informal listening posts exist (e.g., personal observations, conversations with coworkers, stories heard in the community, etc.), a more systematic approach is needed to grasp the true, complete image of your organization and not the desirable, comfortable projection you create.

Patient surveys are one way to gain feedback, but more than one listening post is necessary to gain total awareness. The best performing hospitals used at least four of the techniques described here (note that no one used all of them). The first seven were the most popular.

1. Patient comments

Some hospitals have one or two people read all patient comments and filter them to the appropriate department leaders to make improvements, recognize staff mentioned positively, and track them for evaluations of staff mentioned negatively. Although this tactic has produced good results, it relies heavily upon the assumption that the department leader will actually *do* something with the data.

A more consistently successful approach uses a public, shared commitment to one's peers to make change. Organizations that use this approach (which works in all sizes of hospital) have all department heads gather once a week to review all patient comments together. Patient comments are distributed, and each is read aloud. For positive comments, the manager is expected to note who should be rewarded and recognized for their outstanding performance by, for example, sending them a thank you card personally signed by the CEO, with the patient comment inside. For negative comments, the department leader accepts responsibility for making the necessary changes or improvements to eliminate that cause of dissatisfaction within one week. If the change needed is not obvious, the leader researches the issue by talking to staff, watching the process in action, following up with the patient, etc. At the end of the meeting, everyone has a list of actions that can immediately improve the customer experience. At the beginning of the next meeting, each leader briefly identifies how each item from last week was resolved, and the process starts over.

> ***"Complaint management must be coupled with compliment management"***
> —Director of Patient Services, Greenwich (CT) Hospital

Note that if one person responds to the survey and singles out something specific as a problem, it is likely that many, many more experienced the same problem but did not speak up. Complaining, in person or via survey, is actually a rare event that should be taken seriously.

Because this approach involves continually committing to make an improvement, making that improvement, reporting back, and recommitting to make another improvement in a spirit of perpetual progress, it can change the prevailing culture to a point where championing the patient's cause becomes a valued activity. Organizations using this method have seen the most dramatic improvement trajectory.

2. Patient visits

Hearing a story of a patient's experience firsthand is memorable and, through its emotional resonance, can create a sense of urgency. Patients can be brought in to tell their story to a small group of leaders. Videotaping the visit and story can allow for its strategic reuse and diffusion throughout the organization.

For example, one hospital brought in a patient who was left in tremendous pain in the recovery room for hours. The doctor didn't leave orders for pain medication, and the family was unable to get help because staff were overwhelmed by other patients coming out of surgery. Telling their story to the service excellence council led to the discovery that the recovery room was severely understaffed on certain shifts. The solution was to reschedule staff and to have standing orders for pain meds immediately post-surgery.

3. Follow-up phone calls

Follow-up calls can be used to get more specific feedback and, when appropriate, as a service-recovery opportunity. You could make follow-up phone calls standard so that every patient (or a large percentage of them) receives a call. Ask, "How are things going for you? Do you have any questions? Do you have all of your medications?" before asking about their stay.

However, because this practice is so labor intensive some hospitals limit follow-up calls to instances when they had an extremely low rating in their patient satisfaction survey or received a very negative comment. For example, a survey with "Very Poor" marked for "Response to concerns/complaints" is worth a phone call, if the patient gave his or her number, to politely inquire why. Of course, this call is also a service recovery opportunity.

Consider having people from other departments call regarding distinctive issues. Doing so helps develop cross-functional ties, fosters multidisciplinary perspectives, and can increase the capacity for innovative problem-solving.

4. 24-hour hotline

A hotline provides both patients and staff with an always-available resource to help fulfill virtually any need. Not as many patients use it as one might think, but almost all patients and family members will be comforted by its availability as a safety net.

The hotline should be staffed by exceptionally service-oriented, pleasant, nonclinical personnel who are willing to do anything to fulfill a request. Some organizations use their volunteers to meet needs arising from hotline requests.

To ensure that patients know and use it, promote the hotline intensely: in the admissions material, brochures, tent cards at the bedside, on the phone itself, posters in the rooms and hallways, on the television, in family/visitor information packets, etc.

5. Service quality indicators

Certain measures of clinical quality, such as length of stay, wait times, or bedsores, may also be considered leading indicators of patient satisfaction, and chances are that you're already collecting data for these measures. Listening to these "clinical" indicators can help you improve patient perceptions of quality. For example, a quality improvement intervention that reduces length of stay will likely also produce an increase in patient satisfaction—patients really do want to go home earlier.

6. Formal complaints process

Provide information on your formal complaints process in the admissions packet. By thoroughly explaining the process and potential outcomes, you can manage expectations and establish a powerful perception of fairness. Patients who have a clear understanding of the process will be comforted by the knowledge that they have rights and recourse in this medical encounter—that they aren't completely powerless.

To revolutionize the formal complaints process into a true listening post, examine what you do with all the letters and telephone complaints. Are they categorized and filed away? Are they dumped into a database with canned responses churned out automatically?

7. Complaint tracking database

Using a database that systematically tracks complaints, unsolicited letters, etc., allows you to detect patterns over time. It can show you whether certain areas, staffing levels, or individual clinicians are responsible for a significant volume of the extreme dissatisfaction.

For example, by tracking complaints, one hospital found that parking was a significant problem. They instituted free valet parking, and patient satisfaction increased.

One year of tracking complaints and comments helped another hospital identify lack of quality dining facilities as a major source of aggravation. Tracking these complaints provided support for a proposal to expand the in-house bagel shop into a profitable, full-service restaurant. Complaints stopped, and the hospital actually makes money on the operation.

8. Patient focus groups

Focus groups can serve as a venue for former patients to express their strong feelings regarding a recent visit. They strengthen or rebuild the bonds between patients (and their families) and the hospital. They also can increase positive word-of-mouth as the participants tell others how the hospital listened to them and actually cares about them. Most importantly, you will learn how your patients perceive your service—what they were thinking about when responding to particular questions, what their expectations were at each point during the hospital stay, and any other details peculiar to your geographical area. You also can test their reactions to different services, materials, or interventions to help predict patient reactions. Consider videotaping sessions for use in other training or organizational learning activities.

To ensure that responses aren't positively biased, focus groups should be run by a disinterested third party, such as a patient advocate, university researcher, professional market researcher, or staff from another part of the hospital (e.g., an ambulatory surgery nursing manager could conduct a focus group for an inpatient unit). Remember, the more hospital staff involved in designing and conducting various focus groups, the more they will learn about your patients, other departments, and the overall organization.

9. Patient, family, and community advisory councils

Advisory councils can be convened to analyze specific issues (such as patient rooms, emotional/spiritual care, community health resources, etc.), or a standing council can provide invaluable insight and contribute significantly to the success of initiatives intended to improve patient satisfaction.

10. Mystery shoppers

Mystery shoppers have long been used by service organizations such as hotels and restaurants. Professionals pose as customers and comprehensively examine an organization's service issues (e.g., ease of access, facilities, staff behavior, processes, etc.) and deliver an analysis of their perceptions. Some organizations have found that staff, as well as their friends and family, can be nearly as effective as the professionals. In addition, there is an added benefit—when staff are involved in designing a mystery shopper program, they learn what is being evaluated, which might cause them to improve their behavior immediately.[10]

Note: when reviewing a mystery shopper's analysis remember that it only represents an anecdotal snapshot of one specific time.

11. Suggestion systems

Another listening post is the traditional suggestion box, with a few twists.

First, open it up to staff as well as to patients (in fact, consider implementing it among staff first). Have a team or set of persons formally responsible for rapidly reviewing and implementing the ideas. The approach should emphasize *how can we make this work* instead of *why this just won't work.* Evaluate their efficacy based upon the number of suggestions implemented.

Promote it heavily. Offer rewards for ideas. If an idea saves the organization $50,000, give the person who came up with it a bonus (e.g., $5,000). Allowing people to share in the fiscal success of the hospital and publicly rewarding and recognizing innovations that generate savings will serve as a powerful incentive for everyone to start seriously applying their minds toward improving operational efficiency and patient care.

An alternative to the old-fashioned suggestion box is an intranet-based electronic suggestion box for employees. Assign one person ultimate responsibility for the *entire* process, otherwise long time delays, few results, little publicity, and no accountability can slowly poison the effectiveness of a suggestion system.

PREPARING LEADERS TO RESPOND TO THE RESULTS OF THE LISTENING SYSTEM

Managers may initially rebuff the idea of spending "valuable" time on complaints, suggestions, patient comments, and other listening devices. Nevertheless, a relentless focus on all details related to the patient experience, big and small, is what being "patient-centered" is all about. Prepare them to work on small things. Some of the biggest gains in satisfaction, efficiency, and quality can be made from small changes.

Most of the specific changes customers request are actually quite small. For example, one hospital received a suggestion that they place a hook in the bathroom walls behind the toilet. Managers initially scoffed, debated whether it was worth their time, and openly questioned what possible value little plastic hooks could bring. As it turns out, the IV poles could not fit into the bathroom. If patients wanted to use the toilet (as most of us would naturally prefer), they had to take the IV bag off of the pole and hold it throughout—making for a tricky ordeal and major annoyance.

Many hospitals find that dozens of such small improvements add up to revolutionary gains. "Often large, complex technology and organizations are judged by small details. Attention to the small yields gigantic results. Don't make the mistake of dismissing as inconsequential the small items that customers ask for."[11]

Ideation: Generating ideas and innovations[12]

Gather up improvement suggestions inside the organization. This is the most accessible source of ideation, has the greatest volume, is most quickly obtained, and has the greatest degree of buy-in. The key is to make sure that mechanisms for training and change support are in place before you ask for them, as a high implementation rate is required. In our work, we have sought ideas from these constituencies in this general overlapping order:

Managers. Their ideas include policy and procedure issues. Remove these stumbling blocks for what is to come.

Associates. Sources of a huge volume of ideas that cover every room in the facility, every form, and every patient interaction. They have clinical, nonclinical, and administrative suggestions.

Physicians. We've found that when they first see others actually making change, they become more willing participants. A majority of their suggestions tend to be clinical and customer oriented. We usually work first on irritation removal for them; then we move to the defining of clinical protocols that will affect many other work processes.

Customers. Patient issues first, then friends and family. Usually ideas are lightly solicited from them directly in the first year due to the volume coming in from the earlier sources, many of which directly affect customers. This becomes more of a focused source in year two.

Suppliers. Holding vendors conferences or putting suppliers on project teams is a way to gain what is in essence a free consultancy.

Block 4: Leadership

Demonstrate leadership support. Senior leadership must demonstrate their commitment. As the most visible models, if the leaders at the top are not visibly on board and supportive, staff will lose their morale and motivation for the program. If it doesn't matter to leadership, it won't matter to front-line staff. If there are no consequences for failure to participate wholeheartedly, many won't. For example, at Moses Cone, leadership and management are intimately involved in meeting patients' needs. If a patient waits more than four hours in admission, he or she is visited by the vice president and two directors who each apologize, offer the patient a gift, and leave their card.

One way to demonstrate executive buy-in is their participation in the program launch (e.g., feature in training videos, model behaviors, rounds, etc.). Another way to demonstrate executive buy-in is to make it known to staff that executives, too, participate in the program.

LEADERSHIP SERVICE ROUNDING

This technique is proven to improve communication, awareness, leadership visibility, and both patient and employee satisfaction. The different types of rounding can be categorized as follows:

- Senior leader rounds
- Manager rounds
  - –In your own area
  - –In areas your department serves
- Nurse leader rounds
- Service quality rounds

Senior leader rounding is primarily focused on visibility and communication with employees. Find out what people need, and seek their feedback on anything and everything. Reward and recognize whenever possible. If you've rarely left the office before, staff may take some time to get used to it.

Manager rounding in your own area helps open up channels of communication with your employees. Each department head should round on patients who had recently experienced their service, asking family- and patient-centered questions about the experience, how it can be improved, etc. Any issues brought up should be resolved directly by the manager. The best-performing organizations had managers who took responsibility for gaps in service and immediately resolved them, instead of delegating, putting things on lists for a future date, or forming committees.

Manager rounding in areas your department serves also helps open up channels of communication with your internal customers.

For example, nurse leader rounding is focused on the patient and families on the nursing unit. There is also a secondary benefit to nurse leader rounding: increased visibility and communication with employees.

Service quality rounding is also focused on patients and families in the facility, but not necessarily in your unit.

To do rounding effectively, one must be prepared. It is helpful to practice scripts and role-play responses. Appendix F outlines all of the necessary steps to prepare, track, and implement each of these types of rounding, and Appendix G provides documentation tools. This information is also included in the CD that accompanies this book.

Block 5: Empowerment

For leaders to be successful, they must empower their employees to take on a leadership role within their organization. Trust your people. Grant them authority and hold them accountable. Empowering people gets them to take ownership of the service problems they encounter. It is now their place, their challenge, their department, and their hospital. Empowerment is not about assigning new authority and responsibilities and then walking away—it is about removing barriers.

Because the traditional management model is the opposite of the empowerment model, managers may struggle with the idea. They may not know how to make the shift or are afraid to try. They fear the loss of control, and employees fear the consequences of failure. But in reality, the more management allows employees to make and execute decisions, the more powerful the entire organization becomes.

At its most basic level, empowerment centers on trust and demonstrates how much the organization trusts employees to make and execute decisions. It further illustrates how much employees trust or believe the information allowing them to make and execute decisions.

ARE YOUR EMPLOYEES EMPOWERED?

Empowered employees should be able to answer these questions:

- How far can I bend the rules to satisfy a customer?
- When is it acceptable for me to act without permission?
- At what point is the solution beyond my authority?
- If I require other people's help to solve a customer problem, what protocol do I need to follow to get cooperation?

Everyone must participate in order for empowerment to exist. However, remember that empowerment is a goal that organizations approximate but never quite reach. Organizations can have varying levels of empowerment yet still be successful, as acceptance rates are different and not everybody gets on board at the same time.

Employees often want to take on more responsibility but are afraid to do so. This fear can materialize as resistance. In response, management should continue to push forward by acknowledging and recognizing employees for their progress and slowly widening the boundaries.

WILL EMPLOYEES GIVE TOO MUCH AWAY?

The answer is simple—no. The average expenditure from a service recovery fund is $25. It costs a 250-bed hospital an average of approximately $15,000–$20,000 per year to put a robust service recovery fund in place. For example, Baptist Pensacola empowers all staff with the authority to spend up to $250 on the spot and has not experienced abuse or significant losses. If any patient says that something was lost by the hospital, associates are expected to replace it immediately with cash.

In a nutshell, the more empowered and autonomous employees are, the higher the probability that they will not only meet but also exceed expectations. Empowerment is a self-fulfilling prophecy. The degree to which you empower, trust, strengthen, and serve others is equal to the level that others will rise and deliver high performance and service to the customer.

The manager's empowerment checklist

- ✔ When staff come to you with a problem, instead of solving it for them, ask them, "What do you think should be done?" and then encourage them to execute. There are multiple ways of solving problems. Instead of insisting that people rely on your judgment, encourage staff to grow or develop, or simply engage their ability to judge situations and decide upon the best course of action. Often, being on the front lines puts them in position to make the best judgment.

- ✔ Become your people's coach and champion. Talk up successes, envision the future, help people cope, and do whatever you can to support their needs.

- ✔ Manage like a mentor. Teach, guide, counsel, and challenge. Asking the right questions, being a good listener, and encouraging feedback are signs of an effective mentor.

- ✔ Praise publicly; correct privately.

- ✔ Systematically identify and remove any barriers that prevent staff from acting empowered and independent.

- ✔ Invite the best of your front-line staff to recruit their professional friends whom they think would make good additions to the organization.

- ✔ Tell a story about a time that you didn't succeed at something you prepared for and set out to do (e.g., a presentation). Doing so shows that you are human and that even though you made a mistake, you can use it as a learning experience. This is called empathizing through self-disclosure.

- ✔ Leaders and managers are called to a higher standard. Always do better than the minimum service behavior standards. Always arrive early and stay a little late.

- ✔ Make yourself available. Give staff your personal contact information.

- ✔ Make time outside of the office where you meet with staff to better understand them and their needs. Often, you'll get a lot more information on the culture, work attitudes, problems, and difficulties through discussion in informal settings.

- ✔ Some middle management and supervisors may not react favorably to "their" jobs being diminished. Be aware of these potential feelings of threat and hostility.

TREAT YOUR PEOPLE WITH RESPECT

Management by walking around is not about circulating in the department and saying, "How'ya doing? You're looking nice today." It's getting to know each individual. This means investing 15% of your time to stop and say hello, checking in with each employee, and asking, "What is happening that you would like me to know about?" Have one-on-one meetings with every director to build rapport, talk about their goals, and determine training and education needs.

Give people feedback on things they do well, and things that they aren't doing so well. Recognition is best if it is timely, spontaneous, specific, and geared to that individual.

Empowered employees have the responsibility and authority to meet customers' needs as quickly and effectively as possible. Employees are given the discretion to make day-to-day decisions about job-related activities. By allowing contact employees to make these decisions, the manager relinquishes control over many aspects of the service-delivery process.

This responsiveness is significantly and positively correlated with customer perceptions of service quality and satisfaction. Advocates of empowerment claim that it will allow employees to be more responsive as service providers, be more productive, deal with customer complaints more quickly, be better motivated, and provide higher levels of service quality.[13]

Block 6: Accountability

Improving response to customers' concerns and complaints demands massive decentralization of decision-making power and authority to frontline staff. With empowerment comes accountability. Accountability ensures that concerns or complaints actually get resolved. If staff feel that patients' needs are *always* their responsibility, they will never pass the buck when a patient presents a problem at an inopportune moment.

When a hospital attempts a widespread implementation of a best practice and it fails, the problem is usually a lack of accountability. Your service standards establish clear expectations for behavior; now it is time to enforce them. If someone isn't living up to the standards of performance, talk to them. If unacceptable behavior continues, help them find a job elsewhere. If service standards and service recovery tactics are only given lip service but don't matter in day-to-day operations, the organization essentially relies upon each person's random internal motivation to change their behavior.

Evaluate employees based on compliance with your service behavior standards

There should be zero tolerance for noncompliance with basic customer service behavior standards. Evaluate employees based upon their adherence to the service standards—how many times they are mentioned positively or negatively in patient comments and letters and their department or unit scores for patient satisfaction.

Hospitals may need to completely redesign their performance evaluation to fit the values and behaviors explicated in the standards (or the mission, vision, and values of the organization).

Because standards will be a codified, relatively simple set of concrete behaviors, it is relatively easy to determine compliance with them. Reinforcement through reward and recognition will further solidify the daily behaviors required to succeed in both patient satisfaction and, professionally, for continued employment and promotion. Use empowerment, support, and unambiguous expectations for performance to instill a no-excuses environment where those who aren't on board will either remove themselves or be removed.

Evaluate managers based on compliance with your service behavior standards

Managers also should be evaluated based upon their unit's performance in patient satisfaction, their performance in supporting employee needs (e.g., employee satisfaction or 360-degree feedback), their adherence to the same behaviors (as well as a set of leadership expectations), and their performance in removing irritants/problems identified through committees or patient comments in their area.

It is estimated that 90% of "problem employees" are actually due to a "problem manager." Therefore, it is very important to hold middle managers and supervisors accountable for the way they treat and support their staff.

One hospital made management accountable by making all senior management serve on its Service Excellence Steering Committee, co-chaired by the President/CEO and Director of Patient Satisfaction. They meet weekly and track the problem areas, improvements underway, and hold each other accountable for improving their respective areas. A report on this activity is compiled and published on their intranet, which creates a public structure for accountability. If a problem arises, the meeting automatically provides a forum for transparent and timely decision-making. Because all the department heads are present, the committee can readily make meaningful and accountable changes—an improvement won't die because someone failed to approve something.

"We developed service standards and spoke with people directly . . . everyone had to personally sign that they would follow the standards. One year later, we had to let some people go for not following the standards, especially the attitude standard . . . That really reverberates in an organization."

—Vice President, Baptist Hospital[14]

Block 7: Reliability

Breaking the service promise is the single most important way companies fail their customers. Carelessness, mistakes, and failure to do what someone said would be done, all cause customers to lose confidence in an organization's ability to do what it promises to do dependably and accurately. Reliability is the service "core" to most customers. Little else matters to customers when a company is not dependable.[15]

Reliability is the heart of excellent service. No one wants to be operated on by a surgeon who usually remembers where on the body the surgery is to be done, or to bank with a financial institution that usually keeps its records straight. As consumers we don't find "usually" good enough. If people got things right 99% of the time, there would be nine misspelled words on every page of a magazine and no telephone service for fifteen minutes every day.[16] Even 99.9% isn't good enough; this close to perfection would mean 22,000 checks deducted from the wrong bank account every 60 minutes; 1,314 telephone calls misplaced by telecommunications providers every 60 seconds; and two million documents lost by the IRS annually.[17] We don't tolerate 99.9% service performance in other industries, and we certainly cannot tolerate it in healthcare. Managers should use every opportunity to build a do-it-right-first attitude.

Having reliable employees, reliable upper management, and a reliable service recovery program enables customers to feel that they are entering a safe environment that can be trusted and valued.

Block 8: Teamwork

In helping one another, you also help a patient in the end. If we treat each other as professionals, as colleagues, as team members, and as people who deserve our honesty and respect, the environment becomes one of a team approach. It is no longer "my work," "my job," "my salary," or "my patient." Collaborating brings the expertise of a group of individuals together in order to better serve that patient's needs. If that were your spouse, or your parent, or your sibling or child, wouldn't you want the best care possible for them in the form of a team made up of many different individuals all working for the same cause? We all have areas that we specialize in—why not combine them to create one powerful force?

Block 9: Attitude

Attitude underlies everything. Attitude is how we do things.

Engaging staff in service-recovery efforts can be a challenging process; staff must be willing to assume additional responsibilities and face difficult patient interactions. Vocal support by senior leadership for service principles can strengthen an enterprise-wide effort to provide a better overall experience for patients and visitors, which in turn can boost employee support for service-recovery programs.[18]

Remind staff that the patient could be their parent, spouse, or child and that they should choose the attitude they would want used if the patient was someone they loved and not just another stranger. Encourage them to be compassionate, caring, and enthusiastic even though they may have a tough road ahead. Every day, every shift, they can decide whether to have a positive attitude.

Listen to patient comments on attitude

The person on duty that night was not particularly helpful or friendly. I felt as if I was interrupting her schedule and inconveniencing her.

I feel your staff needs to handle patients more tenderly instead of ignoring them, laughing, joking and being loud at inappropriate times.

The attitude and efficiency of personnel was horrible. It was if we were intruding on them!

None bid you time of day or had smiles . . . most presented with a ho hum attitude like it was just another day and I wasn't important; they appeared unfriendly and unhappy; not what you would expect in a hospital.

Block 10: Recognition

Create visible ways to recognize your staff for providing excellent customer service or for successfully completing the service recovery program. Recognition does not need to be costly to the organization. It could be a matter of mentioning an employee in a public area or at their worksite, posting comments on a board for all employees to view, posting thank you cards sent by senior management, etc. For example, the manager at an admitting department meeting might say, "Our waiting times are decreasing, but what is also important is that when someone waits six hours to get a room, we explain the delay and apologize for it. [Employee's name] is terrific at doing this. Yesterday, she . . ." Publicizing the notable efforts of employees in organizational newsletters provides positive reinforcement and also contributes to the internal marketing of service recovery efforts. For medical staff, the role of the medical director in administering appropriate rewards will be critical. (Samples of simple rewards are included in the CD that accompanies this book.)

Once you have a program in place, it is vital that you come back and revisit the program to evaluate what's working, and what isn't. Rejuvenate your employees by making it fun and keeping it at the forefront of their minds. Establish a program that allows you to be the memory for your patients—they will return the gesture with their loyalty.

Each individual's response to a patient concern or complaint will largely hinge directly upon how their manager/supervisor prioritizes, rewards, and recognizes behavior. Consider how all your leaders, managers, and supervisors treat front-line staff, for they will tend to treat the patients in kind.

The management implications of service recovery

By now, after considering implementing these building blocks as a foundation for a service recovery, it should be clear that service-recovery systems have implications for management.

Like behavior standards, the service-recovery system is fully effective only when all staff are trained, are practiced in, and actually use the process in daily encounters. Getting full participation throughout a large organization is a tremendous undertaking that will require significant time, resources, and dedication. Ensuring daily use/adoption of the practice is equally critical. Improvement in patient satisfaction is unlikely to occur unless a high percentage of front-line staff are actually using your service-recovery practice.

The seminal study of the managerial implications of service recovery in healthcare organizations defined service recovery as that part of quality management designed to alter the negative perceptions of dissatisfied consumers and to ultimately maintain a business relationship with these consumers.[19] The four key findings of that study set the stage for envisioning and crafting your program by providing a solid conceptual framework:

1. Service recovery initiatives can be categorized via two methods of altering perception: psychological and tangible.

2. These methods can be applied to manage perceptions preemptively, concurrently (in instantaneous response to dissatisfaction), and after the fact. For example, a tangible preventive method could be an explicit service warranty, a concurrent method could be to deliver a fruit basket for poor dietary services, and a post hoc method could be to take money off the patient charge. Similarly, a preventive psychological method could be to provide phone access to a patient representative, a concurrent method would be to immediately apologize for a service lapse, and a post hoc method would be to phone the patient at home to apologize.

3. Concurrent service-recovery initiatives require staff to conduct constant surveillance for customer dissatisfaction. Operationally, this would require training staff to listen carefully to the words and observe the actions of customers. Employees who can identify or anticipate existing service problems and sources of dissatisfaction (especially early in their development) are in a position to return a dissatisfied customer to a state of satisfaction.

4. Service-recovery programs that include all hospital employees are in effect holding staff members accountable for performance deficits. Notably, such programs structurally require employees to see the linkage between desirable and undesirable behaviors and attitudes and their consequences. Patients (and family members and friends) do report, by writing on surveys or telling patient relations representatives, the names of staff members whose behavior they found to be either inappropriate or particularly helpful. Our expectation is that soliciting this kind of information should motivate or improve employee performance.

Endnotes

1. Sriram Dasu and Jay Rao, "Nature and Determinants of Customer Expectations of Service, Recovery in Healthcare," *Quality Management in Healthcare* 7, no. 4 (1999): 32–48.

2. *Effective Service Recovery Programs, Original Inquiry Brief,* The Advisory Board Company Washington, DC (May 3, 2004): 2.

3. Dasu and Rao, *supra* note 1.

4. W Boulding W, "A Dynamic Process Model of Service Quality: From Expectations to Behavioral Intentions," *Journal of Marketing Research,* 30 (February 1993): 7–27.

5. Dasu and Rao, *supra* note 1.

6. Torsten Ringberg and Glenn Christensen, "The Influence of Socio-Cultural Frameworks on Consumers' Service Experiences," *Advances in Consumer Research* 30 (2003): 385–386.

7. Kathleen N. Lohr. "Perspective: How Do We Measure Quality? *Health Affairs* 16, no. 3 (May/June 1997): 22.

8. John L. Coulehan, Frederic W. Platt, Barry Egener, Richard Frankel, Chen-Tan Lin, Beth Lown, William H. Salazar, "Let me see if I have this right . . . words that help build empathy," *Ann Intern Med* 135, no. 3 (2001 Aug 7): 221–7.

9. Len Berry, *On Great Service: A Framework for Action* (New York): Free Press, 1995.

10. W. Leebov, G. Scott and L. Olson, *Achieving Impressive Customer Service: 7 strategies for the Health Care Manager* (San Francisco: Jossey Bass, 2000).

11. V. Clayton Sherman. *Raising Standards in American Health Care: Best People, Best Practices, Best Results* (San Francisco: Jossey-Bass, 1999.

12. *Ibid*

13. Peter W. Hom, Michael P. Mokwa, "SERV*OR: A Managerial Measure of Organizational Service-Orientation," *Journal of Retailing,* 74, no. 4 (1998): 461.

14. The Health Care Advisory Board, *Hardwiring for Service Excellence, Hospital Strategies for Breakthrough Improvement in Patient Satisfaction* (Washington DC: The Health Care Advisory Board, 1999).

15. Len Berry, Valerie A. Zeitbaml, A. Parasuraman, "Five Imperatives for Improving Service Quality," *Slogan Management Review* (Summer 1990): 6.

16. *Ibid*

17. N. Gabel, "Is 99.9% Good Enough?" *Training Magazine,* March 1991.

18. *Effective Service Recovery Programs, Original Inquiry Brief,* The Advisory Board Company, Washington, DC (May 3, 2004).

19. S. Schweikhart, S. Strasser, and M. Kennedy, "Service Recovery in Health Services Organizations," *Hospital and Health Systems Administration* 38, no. 4 (1993): 3–21.

CHAPTER 7

THE SIX A'S OF SUCCESSFUL SERVICE RECOVERY ENCOUNTERS

Authors: Kelly Nemeth, Randall S. Blum, Julie Tittle-Plank, Aris Relias-Clark

Every act of service recovery consists of six components: awareness, acknowledgement, apology, active listening, action/amendment/atonement, and avoiding. Some of the steps may happen concurrently.

Awareness

As discussed in Chapter 6, awareness of a problem is one of the basic building blocks of a successful service recovery program. It is also the first step in the individual act of service recovery. And although there are many ways that we can become aware of a specific service failure, you can't just wait until a patient is vocal about the problem—most never speak up.

To discover patients' concerns or problems more often, train staff on what to look for and teach them about the types of problems that can arise. Doing so will allow them to address a problem before it escalates. In addition, emphasize the need to anticipate patient/family problems, and remember that problems that go unnoticed are missed opportunities for improvement.

When educating staff in this area, reinforce your organization's service standards. (See Appendix E for examples of service standards; examples are also included in the CD that accompanies this book.) Any time your service standards are not clearly being met, there is an opportunity. Indeed, one way to differentiate your organization is to empower your staff to respond to concerns before they become complaints. Such empowerment also creates the opportunity to turn what could have been an unpleasant experience into a wow experience.

TIPS FOR BEING AWARE

Be watchful of everything that is going on around you. If there is something that would upset you as a patient, act on it before it becomes a complaint. Taking the initiative when you observe something that might upset a patient is a key part of service recovery.

Scott & White Memorial Hospital in Temple, TX asks that their employees intervene before the patient gets upset. Doing so requires being aware of their surroundings. If employees see a patient waiting for some results and looking a little upset, they might say, "Sir, you seem very anxious about these lab results. Would you like for me to call and find out when they'll be ready?"

Lexington Medical Center in West Cola, SC instituted an automatic service recovery process. Whether there was a complaint or not, every time a department identifies a potential breakdown (such as waiting over a specified period of time, too many needle sticks, or delayed reports), service recovery is automatically activated.

As noted in Chapter 6, rounding is a good way for someone other than the person directly responsible for a patient's care to get pulse checks of what's going on. Rounding by visiting patients lets them know the facility wants to hear if they are having any problems.

AWARENESS OF TELEPHONE ETIQUETTE

Sometimes facilities fail to educate staff on service standards on the telephone. As discussed in Chapter 6, the telephone call is often the first contact patients have with a hospital. That first call is not only an opportunity for a great first impression but it is also a good time to begin molding the expectations the patient should have, to set the stage for the patient, to show good will, and to gain points and trust. Proper phone etiquette is so important that many facilities offer phone training to their staff.

Acknowledgement

Someone expressing a complaint or concern does so precisely because they believe it needs to be acknowledged by someone else. Communicating that you understand the issue does that.

It can be easy to brush aside concerns because action isn't demanded immediately, but this doesn't mean that action won't be demanded in the future—perhaps at an inopportune time. When you acknowledge a concern, you catch an issue that may later become a complaint if left unattended. You take the lead in resolving an issue before it becomes a significant complaint that demands someone's immediate attention.

A concern can be as minor as a comment made in passing. For example, imagine a woman being taken to her room. During the process, she mentioned, almost under her breath, that she would like a cup of coffee. She did not make a big deal about it and certainly never thought (or even expected) that her remark would lead to any action, but imagine her face when her transporter reappears back in her room, five minutes later, with a cup of hot coffee.

Now imagine instead that the patient is, in fact, upset. If that transporter doesn't acknowledge this concern, it could escalate into a complaint because it seems that she isn't being heard. It may be a minor concern, but it can affect the patient's entire mindset and perception of the experience.

Who should acknowledge

It is very easy for people to put their heads down and keep moving, pretending not to notice. Maybe they're due to get off work soon and don't want to start a new project or are in the process of helping someone else. Maybe they just don't want to listen to another complaint. Nonetheless, the organizational culture must be such that anyone who becomes aware of a concern or complaint should stop what they're doing and acknowledge what that patient is going through. A sincere acknowledgement sets the stage for the entire patient experience by creating a positive rapport with the patient.

Consider creating a ten-minute rule

Bothwell Regional Health Center established a "ten-minute rule" in which, when a staff member discovers and acknowledges a concern or complaint, he or she must dedicate at least the first ten minutes to addressing that problem. They own that problem and do everything they can to resolve the issue on their own. If, after the ten minutes has passed, they aren't able to resolve the issue on their own, they are then to seek the help of a manager or supervisor.

Apology

Often an apology is one of the most important gestures staff members can offer a patient. It affirms that someone is truly sorry that the patient endured the particular experience. Unfortunately, something as simple as the apology is often overlooked. Scripts and techniques for delivering sincere, blameless apologies are contained in the CD that accompanies this book.

The blameless apology

Staff are sometimes reluctant to apologize out of fear that if they do so, they are accepting responsibility for the service failure. To help staff overcome this fear, teach them how to deliver a sincere, blameless apology. A blameless apology does not assign blame or say that we are at fault; it simply empathizes with the patient and their situation. Saying, "I am sorry this happened to you," accepts no responsibility for the experience that patient had—it only communicates empathy.

The following are examples of blameless apologies:

"I apologize for the noise in the hallway. I understand why it startled you."

"I am sorry that your food is cold. I would be happy to warm it for you."

"I am sorry your medication has not come from the Pharmacy. Let me see if there is something I can do to expedite it."

"I am sorry that your TV remote is missing. While I look for it, can I help you find something to watch?"

"I am sorry that you did not get the tray you ordered. While I get your requested tray, please feel free to snack on this tray."

"I am sorry that you are dissatisfied with the care you received last night. Please let me know what I can do to make today as pleasant as possible for you."

"I am sorry this happened. I can see why you would be upset. Here's what I'm going to do—. I'll check back in a bit to ensure that everything has been resolved."

"I'm glad that you let me know how important this is to you."

"I apologize for your wait. I realize that waiting is inconvenient. I will keep you informed. Is there anything I can do to make your wait more comfortable?"

"On behalf on the hospital, let me offer this item as a token of appreciation for your patience. We apologize for the inconvenience."

NO ONE SHOULD BE PUNISHED FOR APOLOGIZING

In a culture inundated with the fear of lawsuits, staff may be hesitant to apologize. That's why it's important to send a clear message that the blameless apology is a positive thing and that it's encouraged from top management down. No one will be punished for apologizing. One way to demonstrate this support is to incorporate rewards for service recovery *apologies* into your current recognition program.

THE APOLOGY MUST BE SINCERE

There is an art to apologizing. A canned apology or rote apology can be worse than none at all because it can make it seem like the person is actually mocking the patient.

A good rule of thumb is that, when the problem is very detailed, it is best to summarize it. That is, if the problem can be stated in a few short words, apologize using those short words. For example, consider the patient who has a list of complaints: the computer froze on the admissions staff, the room was not fully prepared, the television's remote control could not be found, etc. If the apology lists all of these experiences, the apology could be perceived as mocking the patient. On the other hand, if the patient pushed the call light to complain because he received the wrong meal tray, then it would be appropriate to say, "I am sorry that you received the wrong meal tray."

Physicians who say they're sorry

Since 2001, several high-profile institutions, including Johns Hopkins Hospital in Baltimore and Dana-Farber Cancer Institute in Boston, have made it policy to urge their physicians to own up to their mistakes and formally apologize. At least two states, Colorado and Oregon, have also passed laws saying an apology can't be used against a doctor in court.

In a case cited in the *Wall Street Journal*, a 50-year-old man developed serious complications about two weeks after his surgery because his doctors left a sponge inside. When the error was discovered, the surgeon told the patient, "No matter how this happened, I was the surgeon in charge; I was the captain of the ship and I was responsible and I apologize for this." Later, an executive of the hospital also apologized. The patient was so impressed with the honesty and candor of the hospital that he didn't even hire a lawyer. The hospital settled directly with him for an undisclosed amount. The patient stated, "They honored me as a human being."[1]

Apologizing tips to remember

- Apologize no matter what the situation or who is at fault. An apology is not about guilt. It is about not having met the customer's expectations.

- Apologize even if you didn't cause the problem.

- When you apologize, you are NOT saying that you are to blame. You ARE saying that you are sorry that the situation occurred.

- An apology conveys your concern, which is what the patient wants to hear.

- Take responsibility for the customer's satisfaction, whether it's the facility's fault or not.

- Don't shift the blame to the customer, another employee, or department.

- Always say *I'm* sorry, not *we're* sorry.

- Apologize at the right time. Don't cut off the patient's explanation or opportunity to fully tell their story. If you throw out apologies left and right without any sense of the person's true experience (as expressed by them), you'll reduce the perceived value and sincerity of the apology.

- Your heart needs to be engaged. An apology cannot be a canned response. Say it like you mean it.

WRITTEN APOLOGIES

An excellent way to follow up after a service failure is to send an apology letter. A letter shows the patient that the issue did not just go in one ear and out the next—the concern was actually communicated to others and is likely being acted upon. Finally, an apology letter sends the message that the organization cares enough to take the time to send them a letter. Below are some examples of scripts for follow-up letters:

"Please accept my apology for the wait time for your test. Your time is important and a lengthy wait can be very frustrating. Enclosed is a gift certificate with our thanks for your patience."

"Please accept our sincere apology for the loss of your watch following your procedure. Enclosed is $40 to replace the item. Thank you for bringing this matter to our attention."

"Please accept my apology for the room move. I can see how frustrating it would be to be asked to make a switch during your stay. Enclosed is a gift certificate for you to enjoy at your leisure with our thanks for your help."

Active listening

As discussed in Chapter 6, active listening is another of the crucial building blocks for a successful service recovery program. It is also vital to the individual act of service recovery.

After the oops, you may get only one shot at making a successful service recovery. If you don't know how to actively listen, you might draw the wrong conclusions and make a service recovery that is less than satisfying to the patient. Here are some tips on how to listen more effectively:

- Give the patient your full attention; stop what you're doing. Focus your attention on the speaker and resist external distractions.

- Introduce yourself at the appropriate time.

- Make contact at eye level, and seat yourself appropriately close to the speaker.

- Restate what you heard. Summarize the patient's comments so that you are sure you understand.

- Set aside prejudices, and don't share your opinion; remain neutral, and see the problem through the customer's eyes, without judgment. You are there to learn what the speaker has to say, not the other way around.

- Do not interrupt. Hear the patient out, and do not rush to speak. Doing so ensures that you get all of the necessary information before reaching a conclusion. Even if it feels uncomfortable to you, allow for silence.

- Remain calm; be aware of your body language and facial expressions.

- Pay attention to the speaker's nonverbal cues.

- Talk in a private area if at all possible.

- Do not blame other people or departments.

- Empathize with the patient. Remember that many people are dealing with health or financial issues, both of which can be very stressful.

- Try not to take the complaint or concern personally.

- Review mentally what you already know about the subject.

- Don't agree or disagree; rather, encourage the train of thought.

- Be involved. Actively respond to questions and directions. Use your body position (e.g., lean forward) and pay attention to encourage the speaker and signal your interest.

LISTENING ROUNDS AND AMBASSADOR PROGRAMS

Duke University Hospital launched an initiative that required a unit or department leader to visit each patient within the first 24 hours of admission or transfer. Although few patients expressed concerns during the visit, the majority expressed appreciation that someone was willing to listen and follow up on any concerns. After just three months of such visits, Duke saw a dramatic rise in patient satisfaction with staff response to concerns and complaints.

Listening is a vital component of any patient rounding program. Listen, ask questions, respond honestly and openly to concerns, and ask for advice on how to improve services or add missing services. This will allow you to identify medical, psychological, spiritual, and discharge issues that can be addressed immediately, not to mention systemic issues that require intervention.

Ambassador and greeter programs are also gaining popularity, and listening is an essential ingredient in the success of these programs. These programs are most successful when the ambassadors or greeters are outgoing individuals who have good communication skills and who have been trained in listening skills. Of course, they also must be empowered to execute the requests of patients. Caring, compassion, and listening are key.

If you take the time to give the patient your full attention, remain neutral rather than getting emotionally involved, and empathize with them, a lot of misunderstandings can be avoided, and you can be on your way to making successful service recovery.

Action, amendment, atonement

Sometimes an apology isn't enough; patients want action. They want to know that something is being done to correct the problem. In such a case, let the patient know that you appreciate the feedback and make sure that he or she is kept up to speed on the progress. Follow these six steps:

1. Make it easy for a patient to complain. Inform patients and their families of their right to make a complaint. Give them the number of your guest or patient relations department in case any issues arise during their stay. Train your staff to read non-verbal clues, and encourage them to be proactive. Remember few dissatisfied patients actually complain. Reading non-verbal clues can help to identify these silent dissatisfied patients and give you a chance to correct the issue before the patient leaves.

2. Acknowledge that the patients are important and that their feedback is valuable. Allow them to express their frustration. Often this is the most important part of the process—it ensures that you get all of the necessary information before reaching a conclusion. Make sure to validate what the person is saying. Doing so reduces patients' anger and lets them know you want to help. Offer a sincere apology, whether in person, by phone, or by mail. Doing so will speak volumes.

3. Ensure that the patient only has to explain his or her concerns once and to one person. Implement a ten-minute rule: When you discover a service recovery opportunity, you own the problem for the first ten minutes. During those first ten minutes, do everything you can to resolve the problem. After ten minutes, seek assistance as needed from a supervisor or manager. When talking to the patient, ask open-ended question that begin with "What," "How," "Why," and "Tell me about . . ." Restate what the customer says. Doing so allows you to check for understanding and lets the patient know that you are listening. Be sure to write down vital information and read each point back to demonstrate concern for getting it right.

4. Provide patients with clear consistent information to answer all my questions—if you cannot answer a question, either get the answer for them or ask someone who can. Before leaving, ask if the patient has any other questions.

5. Investigate the problem quickly—Be sure to explain what you are going to do. Let the patient know how you will follow up: "I'll be back to check that . . ." or "I will make sure you get your food tray."

6. Resolve the problem fairly and involve the patient in the solution. If possible, give the patient options: "This is what we can do . . ." Offer a fair fix. If warranted, offer a small token appropriate to the patient's concern, such as free parking passes, gift certificates to the gift shop, and phone cards. Follow up! Confirm with patients that their concerns have been resolved and that you care. Thank them again for sharing their concerns. Before leaving, ask, "Is there anything else I can do for you now?"

Avoiding

To sustain success staff must learn how to prevent the same problems from reoccurring in the future and anticipate possible new problems.

Put a tracking system in place so you are not recovering from the same problem over and over again. All complaints, no matter the size or severity, should be logged in a central database to track trends and identify underlying problems. Staff must understand the importance of doing this, and that logging the complaint is also a step in the individual act of service recovery.
Ideally, the tracking program will allow you to be proactive with problems.

For example, through complaint tracking, one ED was able to identify that, when it was very busy, a common complaint was that patients and family members were thirsty and hungry. To respond to this problem, the facility had a volunteer walk around with a snack cart during their busy periods. Although this was not a very costly initiative, it was very rewarding. The feedback that they received was very positive.

Any system you use should track not only the problems that a facility is recovering from but also the gift distribution. The system should track what types of gifts are offered in what types of situations. In addition to showing whether the service recovery program is being used, tracking gifts will help a facility to budget appropriately for next year. It also will help with training and re-evaluating our program.

The CD that accompanies this book contains additional example of tracking forms and log, and an Excel® spreadsheet for tracking service recovery.

Initially, it is not uncommon to experience an increase in complaints, as customers become accustomed to your willingness to hear negative comments and suggestions for improvements. Over time, however, if you are truly customer-driven, complaints should decrease and satisfaction should increase.

Tips for avoiding the same problem over and over

- Ask yourself, "What needs to be done to prevent this from happening again? What can I do to help?" The goal is to make sure that all bases are covered.

- After you think the problem has been resolved, follow up with the patient to make sure that is the case. Ask them, "Is there anything else that I can do?" If the patient does not feel that the problem was resolved to their satisfaction, they will likely bring it to the attention of someone else.

- Make sure that you communicate to the patient what is being done to prevent this problem from occurring in the future. If a patient does not feel that the proper steps are taken to ensure that someone else doesn't go through this experience, they will likely complain again.

Figure 7.1

Service recovery form

SERVICE RECOVERY FORM

Date: ______________

Demographic Information

Complainant's Name: ________________________ Room #: ____________________

Home Phone #: ______________________________ POA Phone #: ________________

Account #: _________________________________ Medical Record #: ____________

Complaint Description

_ Delay of 1 hour
_ TV problems
_ Parking
_ Excessive noise
_ Staff attitude
_ Multiple bed transfers
_ Billing issues
_ Unanswered call light
_ Uncoordinated services
_ Failure to follow-up/communicate MD___ Nurse___
_ Processing delays
_ Care issues
_ Multiple Issues (please describe below)

____

____

____

____

(If additional space required, complete on separate page and attach to form)

Severity level of complaint

_ High
_ Moderate
_ Low

Item

_ Fruit basket
_ Gift shop flower bouquet
_ Restaurant gift certificate
_ Parking voucher

Follow-up Required

_ Yes
_ No

Follow-up Information

Date of follow-up_____________ By Whom_________________________________

Outcome____

____

____

Employee Information

Name__________________________ Department______________________________

Supervisor____

Employee Signature____

Case study: How one hospital did it

Sarasota Memorial Health Care System (SMH) is the second largest public hospital in Florida. It is among the top national providers of open-heart surgery and the third largest cardiac provider in Florida. SMH has 685 physicians on its medical staff and employs approximately 3,000 people.

CULTURE CHANGE

Creating culture change—that is, a palpable difference in the way members of the organization interact and the shared values they hold—is often the hardest task. SMH started this process with a strategic-planning gathering of all key stakeholders in the hospital to determine a new mission, vision, and values. Together, key hospital board members, administrators, physicians, nurses, community members, and other employees re-visioned the hospital's direction.

Among the goals for organization culture change was to create a culture of accountability by dealing directly with the brutal facts, honestly communicating, and laying everything on the table for employees.

Based upon the scorecard which balanced service, quality, people, financial, and growth factors, several structures for accountability were instituted:

- Each leader had to submit a 90-day plan on what he or she will be doing along the SMH five pillars.
- The first 90-day plan out was the CEO's and was e-mailed to everyone.
- All leaders in the organization wee publicly accountable for their 90-day plans.
- Evaluations are no longer subjective.
- Each leader received a quarterly report card with goals and evaluations under each pillar.
- Merit raises were entirely dependent upon meeting all goals on the balanced scorecard.

Every Monday at 1:00 p.m., the leadership team gathered and read all of the patient comments from the surveys. Risk management followed up on extremely negative surveys. (Risk management had always tracked patient complaints to determine whether the complaint was a clinical quality problem or a customer service problem.) Each leader accepted responsibility and took actions based upon the negatives. Positive comments were posted publicly in the appropriate areas.

Another goal was to create a non-punitive culture. In the previous environment, people were afraid not only of making mistakes but also of pointing out the mistakes of others or coming forward when they themselves made mistakes.

BEHAVIOR STANDARDS

Customer satisfaction teams were formed because there was the perception that administrators only cared about cutting costs. Teams included inpatient, outpatient, emergency care, standards, measurement/communication, service recovery, reward and recognition, and physician satisfaction. With the input of all employees, the customer satisfaction teams developed the following four universal behavior standards to which all employees were expected to adhere:

- Always make a positive impression.
- Make communication effective.
- Practice professionalism and excellence with a team-centered approach.
- Develop and use service recovery skills.

All employees were given a handbook that explained the standards and the philosophy underlying them. These behaviors were not optional; they were a condition of employment. Everyone had to sign an agreement to practice and adopt the standards.

KEY PHRASES

Is there anything else I can do for you? OR I've got some time right now—is there anything I can do for you while I'm here?

By having all staff ask patients and family members this question as they leave the room, questions/concerns/complaints can be addressed immediately, without allowing them to fester or rise up at a less opportune time for nurses. Sarasota found that most patients didn't make any requests, and those that did (10%–20%) usually wanted something minor that didn't require a nurse. Thus, having all staff ask the question freed up nurses to provide complex medical care.

Both behavior standards and key phrases were integrated into employee evaluations. And because the behaviors and standards were determined by staff, SMH didn't need to send out a memo about them.

Employee satisfaction

SMH's leaders believed that front-line staff would never buy into these standards and practice them unless they were satisfied with and believed in the hospital. However, many employees were publicly bashing the hospital—the hospital was only one year removed from layoffs and nurses picketing the hospital.

To address this issue, leadership focused on "Level of pride felt" and "Encourage your friends to apply for work at Sarasota Memorial" as leading indicators of turnover and culture. They used recognition and reward as the primary mechanisms for improving employee satisfaction. Many resources were made available to allow leaders to systematically reward and recognize employees including, customer service hero awards and mass quantities of individualized recognition.

Service recovery program

SMH used to tell staff to never apologize for anything, so it was a big cultural shift to learn to apologize—and to learn to thank people for bringing a complaint. Take Heart was an acronym for the following:

Hear the complaint
Empathize and evaluate
Apologize
Resolve
Thank them

Staff learned and practiced the blameless apology. Culturally, leadership emphasized not bad-mouthing other departments and other staff. They reminded everyone that the patient doesn't care about departments and sees everyone as one big team. If people bad-mouthed others, the patient didn't like it and, worse yet, began to wonder whether there were safety issues.

Rounding

Before instituting this program, the only time anyone saw leadership or senior management on the floors was when something went wrong. Now, senior management rounded in their own departments, in other departments, and on new patients. Different leaders rounded on different days.

The most important part of rounding was going to see the nursing leaders. Thus, leaders rounded with their employees first, then with the patients—not necessarily all patients, but certainly with the new patients and service recovery patients. Rounding to meet employees' needs, even the simplest ones, was critical to improving both employee and patient satisfaction.

HIRING PROCESS AND SELECTIVE RETENTION OF STAFF

Once the program was in place, everyone was hired for their customer service aptitude and trained for whatever technical skills they need. Of course, for nurses, certain basic clinical skills were also required. The hiring process also used peer interviewing as a way to evaluate candidates for their customer service disposition. Volunteers were also selectively "hired" and trained with customer service skills, like employees. More than 1,000 volunteers logged more than 160,000 hours rounding on patient and families.

New employees were now given an in-depth orientation on customer service, behavior standards, and the organization's balanced approach at hire. For the first 90 days, new employees wore a star on their badge so people are aware that the employee is new.

After 90 days, a second evaluation occurred, and sometimes newly hired individuals would be eliminated. Many left of their own accord because they couldn't handle the customer-centric ethos. Those that stayed on were given a follow-up orientation at 90 days to reinforce the cultural values, expectations, and behaviors.

Among the brutal facts that SMH had to address was that low performers weighed them down. Employees who performed below expectations in employee evaluations were asked to find jobs elsewhere.

SPECIAL CONSIDERATION FOR FOOD SERVICE PERSONNEL

In addition to the four universal behavior standards, food service personnel had some job-specific behaviors to learn. For example, in addition to simply delivering the food, waiters were expected to obtain the condiments and utensils, open containers, pour drinks, and resolve problems with the meal on the spot. They even read the menu aloud for the next meal and solicited individual preferences. The nursing staff noticed the difference: When food service staff started to do this, it freed up their time to provide for patient pressing medical needs.

The hiring process described above also applies to food service personnel, but to an even greater extent. They are hired solely on customer service and will train for whatever technical skills are needed.

Finally, food service took these standards to the next level by changing the menu, aspects of service and processes to meet and resolve patient comments and complaints. This included requiring food service waiters to wear tuxedo shirts, cummerbunds, and black trousers.

CHANGE IN INTERNAL COMMUNICATION INFRASTRUCTURE

The original communication infrastructure for service quality improvement was characterized by a lack of meaningful data, direction, and teamwork. Despite having three full-time employees dedicated to communicating and disseminating patient satisfaction data, results were shared only quarterly and organization-wide results were never tied into department-specific results and often created confusion.

SMH was doing what it now considers to be all the wrong things when internally communicating results, including the following:

- Only sharing scores and reports quarterly
- Disconnecting department-specific results from organizational results
- Not sharing information with front-line staff or, at the other extreme, sharing too much with them, putting them on information overload
- Only giving mean scores (in contrast, a percentile ranking would have shown massive effects of small movements in scores)

Today, the situation is different:

- The strategic planning unit developed a single intranet site for all strategic goals, objectives, and data, which is continually updated as soon as they became available.

- The information systems department ensured that all areas had up-to-date computers and software to allow everyone access to the information.

- Reports are tailored to specific departments and user groups within that department and tied to the organization's overall objectives and goals.

- Graphical interpretation of the results is used to simplify the reports and make them easier to understand.

- All results are presented, including financial data. The first time this was done marked the beginning of a no-secrets culture and information-sharing ethos.

- A weekly President's Page newsletter is sent to all employees via e-mail.

- Formal invitations are sent to staff at home to listen to the president every quarter at an open forum. The CEO and senior leaders hold multiple open forums for employees to discuss the hospital's situation and update the status of goals across the balanced scorecard. Employees can ask any questions they have—nothing is considered off-limits. To get people to come to the forum, the organizers hold drawings for prizes and gift certificates.

- The CEO attends the 90-day follow-up orientation explicitly to obtain feedback from new employees on what the hospital is doing and what it can be doing better.

OTHER CHANGES

Employee thank you-notes and phone calls

Every patient was mailed a card signed by the nurses who cared for that patient.

Nurses initially resisted making discharge phone calls, insisting that they didn't have time. However, when leadership made it clear that this was not optional, they found they could make it happen.

Free valet parking

In response to numerous complaints about the scarcity of parking, free valet parking was introduced. The valet was trained to help the patient into a wheelchair and to park the car while the driver helped the patient from that point on.

Elevator etiquette

Patients on gurneys now get the elevator to themselves and their medical attendant—no one else is allowed on. This practice eliminates the prying eyes of strangers.

Leadership institute

An educational program was designed to help senior managers gain the competencies needed to achieve superior results in employee satisfaction, customer service, finance, physician relations, strategic planning, and goal setting. It included important interpersonal communication skills and ongoing leadership training and career development to boost retention and recruitment.

Managers receive similar training in the leadership institute but focused on supervisory skills and day-to-day operations.

OUTCOMES

Patient satisfaction with staff response to concerns and complaints rose dramatically. Overall, patient satisfaction percentile rank increased from 15th percentile in the second quarter of 1999 to the 90th percentile by September 2001.

Overall net income rose from $2.2 million loss in fiscal year 1998 to $14.9 million positive operating margin in fiscal year 2001, for a total increase of $16.1 million in three years.

Employee turnover fell from 25.2% to 17.5%.

Endnote

1. Charles S. Lauer, "To Err is Human: And a heartfelt apology might be just what the doctor ordered to head off lawsuits," *Modern Healthcare* (May 24, 2004): 20.

PART IV

PROGRAMS

CHAPTER 8

BEST PROGRAMS, BEST PRACTICES

Scott Holmlund, Tracey K. Doubrava, Richard A. Jun, Barbara S. Van Holsbeke

In 2004, Press Ganey issued a call to more than 4,000 partners to discover the best active service recovery programs. From this research, we determined certain best practices that were common to all successful service recovery programs. Although all service recovery programs are unique and call for constant creativity and innovation, the programs and best practices outlined in this chapter give you a world-class place to start.

- Empower employees.
- Gather the team.
- Set a theme.
- Introduce the program.
- Educate and train.
- Create a toolkit.
- Provide scripting.
- Reward and recognize.
- Track and trend.

Empower employees

In a patient-focused facility, service recovery is a natural extension of ensuring that each patient experience is favorable. A service failure presents an opportunity to transform a dissatisfied customer into a wowed customer. To do so, staff must be empowered—empowered to recognize and acknowledge the failure, empowered to apologize for the mistake, empowered to fix the situation, and empowered to turn the moment of dissatisfaction into a "wow." In other words, the staff are able to make it right.

Each and every staff member must know that, despite best efforts, mistakes will occur. This knowledge will give them the confidence to take responsibility and apologize for the failure if there is organization buy-in. Staff should be trained at hire and then on an ongoing basis about how to engage the dissatisfied customer and how to determine an effective and agreeable resolution.

JUST ONE SIGNATURE

At Lexington Medical Centers (LMC) (West Columbia, SC) staff members know that *it only takes one signature*—theirs—to get an item from the gift shop for a patient, family member, or visitor who has a concern or complaint about the care experience. The basis for their service recovery program comes down to empowerment. LMC believes that if associates are capable of making decisions that will significantly affect patients' well-being, they are also capable of deciding how to mend a service relationship that needs fixing.

AN EMPOWERMENT STATEMENT

At Western Maryland Health System (Cumberland, MD), the entire staff learns the "Empowerment Statement" as part of their training. Quite simply, the empowerment statement says the following to staff:

- *You* are the right person to take charge of handling the customers' concerns.
- *You* should respond to the patient as if you were the patient.
- *You* are our organization—the goodwill ambassador who can make or break our reputation.

Sessions are held to teach employees that the key to superior service quality is that each employee is empowered to perform service recovery. The empowerment statement is part of the training presentation.

Gather the team

Recovery Discovery

Responsible means response-able or able to respond. Enabling someone to respond makes that person responsible.

A recurring thread among hospitals that submitted their programs to Press Ganey was the importance of selecting a multidisciplinary group of excited people who have a passion for service excellence. Forming a powerful and dynamic group as your steering committee is the first step on the road to a successful service recovery program because this team heads up the change-management business. Instituting large-scale cultural change requires passion and desire throughout the entire organization. After all, service recovery is every person's responsibility.

INVOLVE LOTS OF PEOPLE

It is almost impossible to involve too many people. The more people involved, the greater the buy-in and enthusiasm, and the more diverse and useful the feedback. For example, when Lexington Medical Center identified patient satisfaction as an issue and realized that it needed to improve its service recovery process, it formed a service recovery team composed of representatives from nursing, engineering, environmental services, nutrition services, guest services, and staff development.

Team members interviewed front-line staff to identify scenarios and processes with the greatest potential for service breakdown. Because team members came from different areas of the hospital, staff felt more comfortable talking—there was likely to be someone who was familiar with their work.

Western Maryland Health Systems began with a steering committee of ten members. In designing and implementing their program, the steering committee ultimately enlisted more than 120 enthusiastic people from all over the organization. This was, in part, because as their process developed (initially, their focus was exclusively on inpatient issues), they realized that service recovery was a process that could be used in all their facilities, including several outpatient surgery centers, urgent care centers, and physician practices.

Recovery Discovery

Recruit your team strategically. Although power is important, don't just pick managers. Look for service-recovery champions who will tirelessly promote the cultural change. Find persons who want to differentiate themselves and who will take on additional responsibility. Select people who will not be deterred by the obstacles that will arise even with the best-laid plans.

Having a large number of people involved not only rallies a large team but also includes many people in the process who might otherwise sit on the sidelines. Remember, the more people who have ownership in the program, the more quickly you begin to change the culture of the organization.

Even those players who may not have been the first ones picked for the team can bring excitement and enthusiasm that is contagious for the whole team. These people are throughout your organization in places that you might have overlooked. Search for the maintenance person who brings a kind word to everyone he passes by, or the technician who gives directions to visitors that look lost. These are also the people who will ensure a successful service recovery team.

SET GOALS

The service recovery team sets the goals for the program, but these goals must be consistent with your organization's global culture. Goals should not be selected without careful deliberation. The form on the facing page lists some questions a team should consider as it reflects on possible goals. Remember, everyone on the team has to accept the goals and believe that they can be accomplished.

There are several basic rules when setting service recovery (or any) goals:

Goals must be measurable

You must be able to measure progress, and you must set goals that are realistic and attainable, not pie-in-the-sky ideals that will frustrate all involved if you fall short of them.

Set realistic time frames

Use realistic time frames when tracking progress; do not expect success overnight. For example, Sharp Metropolitan Medical Campus (San Diego, CA) sets and achieves goals in ninety-day increments. The team develops action plans, and then each quarter, the action plans and a report on their successes are presented to the action team leaders.

Use goals to set priorities

When your service recovery team sets goals, it helps align performance by focusing staff. Goals provide a mechanism to recognize efforts and reward achievement. Goals dictate the priorities your team will work on and facilitate for the rest of the staff.

Team members research best practices and evaluate various approaches to service recovery; then a customized program can be drawn up. The service recovery team sends helpful hints to managers, shares ideas, and even dispels myths. This can be done using the facility's intranet, e-mails, or posters. The team must also keep coming back to rejuvenate the process and keep the education level and motivation high.

Reflecting and deliberating on goal setting

1. What do you know about goal setting?

2. What goal have you set?

3. What are your concerns about goal setting?

4. What is the current performance of the department/area? What are the reasons for performance at this level? Do you think you can do better? Do department employees think they can do better? Why? Is it important for nondepartment employees to see improvement in this area? Why?

5. Why is a goal being proposed? How does the current performance of the department/unit/area relate to the current performance of the organization? Is the current performance acceptable or unacceptable? What are the highest scores achieved in peer groups of like-facilities and units?

6. Is your organization committed to patient satisfaction as an important value? Does everyone believe that improved patient satisfaction is a priority? What will happen if satisfaction improves? What are the rewards or benefits? What will happen if "nothing happens"?

7. What are you going to do to achieve your goal? (*This is the critical aspect of goal setting that many clients don't quite understand. The ability to achieve whatever goal they set is contingent upon changing/improving patient experiences. It's important to see that many things need to happen across the entire organization to radically change patient experiences*.)

8. Specifically, what plans do you have to develop (and implement) a customer service infrastructure? Do you currently have a set of "Service Standards"?

9. How will your organization hold employees and leaders accountable for consistently demonstrating your organization's "Service Standards"?

10. What is your current process for training existing employees? New hires?

11. What other metrics (e.g., leading indicators) will you use to determine whether your changes in structures and processes are improving patient experiences?

12. Are there areas/processes that are widely known as patient dissatisfiers? Have any steps been taken to correct these dissatisfiers? What will be different in the coming year?

13. What major events are planned at the organization, particularly those that affect employee morale? Are you redesigning a service line, moving a facility, constructing an addition, or going into a merger?

14. Have you considered potential pitfalls that may occur this year? What events are likely to occur that will create "push-back" against your initiatives? What will you do to overcome this push-back?

15. List 20 things that you are going to change or do differently. Ask yourself and others whether making these changes will ensure that patient satisfaction will increase.

Set a theme

Another best practice is the creation of a theme. This theme should be meaningful, memorable, and reinforcing. A good theme underscores the core elements of your program and serves as a reminder to all levels of staff that the patient is the customer and that every effort should be made to correct any deficiencies in service.

When naming your service recovery program, try to develop a theme using words that everyone will remember. Create acronyms that are clever, memorable names, with each letter representing a step in the service recovery process. Alternatively, use a series of the same letters with each letter representing a keyword in the process.

The theme or acronym you choose should be displayed prominently. Use it on posters, in presentations, and on reminder cards, apology cards, bookmarks, flyers, or mugs. Some service recovery teams give pop quizzes to staff about their service recovery theme during special rounding sessions. Exposure, encouragement, and rewards help obtain desired staff participation.

ACRONYM THEMES

ACT

Sharp Metropolitan Medical Campus uses the acronym ACT for their program.

Acknowledge and apologize with no excuses.

Correct the issue or make it right.

Take action or take it forward.

Sharp plays with this acronym by inviting employees to catch others in the ACT of caring. Employees who were caught in the ACT are then rewarded for their service recovery efforts. The theme showed up in other areas, such as, "Be proACTive rather than reactive," "Learn to take ACTion," "ACTions speak louder than words," "ACTion before reACTion," and "Service recovery is an ACT of kindness."

GIFT

Lexington Medical Center uses GIFT as its theme.

Give a sincere apology.

Inform the customer.

Fix the problem.

Thank the customer.

Lexington used this theme because they view complaints as a gift. They used service recovery GIFT boxes on each unit with gifts inside. They ran a contest with GIFTS of free lunches to the employees who used the program. The unit with the most usage based on bed capacity received a GIFT for their unit, and one person's name would be drawn for a GIFT of eight hours paid time off.

RELATE
At Jefferson Regional Medical Center (Pittsburgh, PA), you will hear about the RELATE program:
Recognize the problem.
Empathize with the customer.
Listen closely and pay attention.
Apologize.
Take action to correct the problem.
Explain.

Jefferson used posters to emphasize the standard of the month. Staff members were given bookmarks with the RELATE steps on one side and service recovery tips on the other side. Each step is addressed in their training session.

CARE
Both Women & Infants Hospital (Providence, RI) and Russell Medical Center (Alexander City, AL) use this acronym.
Connect with the customer.
Apologize and thank the customer.
Resolve the situation/fix the problem.
Evaluate to determine whether the efforts have been successful.

At Women & Infants' Hospital, "Because We CARE" gift cards are printed in English on one side and in Spanish on the other side. They survey users to evaluate the CARE program.

STAR
If you want to become a STAR, follow the steps from Henry Ford Wyandotte Hospital (Wyandotte, MI).
Show concern and listen.
Take ownership and see the issue to the end.

Apologize, regardless of the situation.
Resolve the problem so it doesn't recur.

Have **A HEART**
Have A HEART is the theme used at Southern Ohio Medical Center (Portsmouth, OH).
Apologize.
Hear them out.
Empathize.
Ask questions.
Respond.
Thank the customer.

ERASE *unsatisfactory service experiences*
St. Luke's Hospital and Health Network (Bethlehem, PA) uses the acronym ERASE for their program.
Evaluate or examine the situation.
Regrets are expressed.
Act immediately to correct the situation.
Satisfy the customer's needs.
Evaluate the effectiveness of the recovery.

St. Luke's makes it their goal to ERASE unsatisfactory service experiences. They evaluate the effectiveness of recovery and eliminate future occurrences.

USE A SERIES OF LETTERS

Three* R*'s
Every good student knows his or her three R's, and it is no different at Western Maryland Health System. They use the three R's as the theme for their program.
Recognize; listen and confirm accuracy.
React; blameless apology, avoid defensiveness.
Rectify; apology card or gift.

Four* A*'s
Bothwell Regional Health Center (Sedalia, MO) uses AAAA.
Acknowledge/listen/take notes

Apologize; provide blameless apology
Amend; fix the problem quickly and fairly
Atone; offer a physical token of apology

The* A *Team
Genesis Medical Center (Davenport, IA), invites all of their staff members to be part of the "A Team."
Awareness of the problem.
Acknowledge the mistake.
Apologize. **A**ctively listen.
Act to amend.

Introduce the program to your staff

Ceremonies serve the purpose of introducing new relationships. They provide visible proof that the organization is making a commitment. Introducing a service recovery program means that those involved share a common vision of taking care of their patients. A ceremony will acknowledge that coming together toward a goal. Introducing your service recovery program to your staff is a tool to get people involved and excited, and it communicates the message of your commitment.

One of the goals of your introduction ceremony is to include all members of the organization and communicate the direction of the program. This is your time to inspire and educate staff. Make it a great kickoff, with posters hung up around the facility, stories in newsletters, and contests to generate interest.

HOLD A GAME DAY
Holzer Medical Center (Gallipolis, OH) held a game day for their employees. The theme was opening day at the baseball field. A conference room was set up to resemble a baseball diamond with a display at each base. A team member was on each base to describe the steps of the process using the acronym for their theme, HANDS:

First base = **H**ear
Second base = **A**pologize
Third base = **N**eed to Act
Pitcher's mound = **D**emonstrate the Holzer Difference
Home plate = **S**uccessful service recovery

Foul balls and errors were discussed because they are inevitable and employees need to know what it takes to recover. After the successful kickoff, flyers were posted throughout the facility with the HANDS process illustrated because Holzer felt that repeated exposure was the best way to improve familiarity.

HAVE A CONTEST

Henry Ford Wyandotte Hospital used a contest to make its service recovery rollout fun. The facility has treasure chests to hold service recovery tools, such as gift vouchers and tracking slips. Decorated treasure chests were brought to the celebration to be judged and winners were announced.

Educate and train

Service recovery programs are a great idea, but without initial and ongoing education and training, all your efforts may turn into glorified lip service. Your program will be headed for failure if you give your staff tools without guidance. (The CD that accompanies this book provides examples from some of the education and training programs discussed below.)

The education and training aspect of your service recovery program can be approached informally. You can begin the educational process through word-of-mouth. This process should begin with staff talking about the developing program, which will generate interest. The service recovery team should share what they are working on and invite input. Internal marketing of the program happens when an intranet or internal posting system is used to post an article on the concept of service recovery.

Formal training includes staff at every level of the organization. Members of the senior leadership team should address the staff to explain the concept of a service recovery program and publicly affirm their buy-in. Staff should come away with an understanding that, although mistakes happen, their responses to such mistakes is what is the key to the program's success. Moreover, staff should understand that from now on they will be rewarded and recognized for their efforts.

Formal training should include concrete examples of service failures. Such examples convey the importance of acknowledging the mistake and taking ownership of it with an apology, display all available resources to fix the problem, and emphasize why it is so important to go the extra step to wow the patients. Role-playing and scripting are effective teaching techniques.

The same points covered in initial trainings should be reinforced with follow-up and ongoing training. One way to reinforce the training and the hospital's support of the program would be small group meetings in which incidents are openly discussed. Staff should feel free to share effective uses of the program and to discuss instances when a service failure was overlooked or not handled as well as possible. This ongoing training also should allow staff to express discomfort or frustration. Just as we want our customers to share their complaints, we also need staff to tell us their feelings. If any element of the program is not working for staff, that issue must be addressed.

COMMUNICATION TRAINING

Changing the way people communicate can be challenging. It requires continual reinforcement and practice. One presentation, one time, will not work. In fact, as the science of organizational learning has advanced, we now understand that lectures and formal presentations are the least effective learning method.

Orientation training can range from eight hours to upward of six days. For example, Memorial Hospital Pembroke's (FL) approach to orientation training simply and systematically lays the groundwork for the basics of patient satisfaction and then the remainder of the training emphasizes teamwork, communication, and response to concerns/complaints.

Continuous training for customer service, service recovery, and, especially, empathetic communication can range from eight hours every quarter to 10 hours a month, to a top allocation of 14 different day-long sessions per year. Regardless of how organizations arranged their training, all of them prioritized continuous learning, situation-specific training sessions (in addition to larger training initiatives), and outcomes.

Training methodologies that high-performers and top-improvers found effective in achieving the goal of actual adoption and practice of service recovery behaviors include the following:

- Building service recovery training upon a solid foundation of basic training in customer service skills. For an example of how Memorial Hospital Pembroke did this, see the box on p. 128.

- Practicing key phrases.
  - Practice the blameless apology.
  - Videotape role-plays or practice communications. Role the videotape back. Watch for clarity, tone of voice, confidence, empathy, and body language.

– Laminate pocket cards with key phrases.
– Ask staff, "What do you say that seems to work in responding to customer needs?"

- Role-playing.
  - Role-play a different customer encounter every day at the start of the shift. It only takes five to 10 minutes, but add it up and you get 30–60 hours of active training practice. Staff really enjoy this because it provides an opportunity to raise situations they encountered and see how others would handle it. "I had this customer yesterday. Here's what I did. How would you have handled it?"
  - At every team meeting, say, "Tell me about a service recovery situation that went well."

- Using standardized patients.
  - Tap into the expertise of any academic affiliations you may have (or develop a training partnership) to use standardized patients in your training. Standardized patients are professional actors on whom medical students practice.
  - Videotape the encounter and review it with staff and the standardized patient. Ask participants what they were feeling at different moments, what worked, and what didn't.

- Developing your own series of training videos.
  - Keep them to less than 15 minutes to encourage everyone to use them as a part of regular staff meetings.
  - Keep it simple and fun.
  - Involve people from your organization in the video. Seeing a CEO or some other high-profile leader in a funny situation can be quite memorable.
  - Reinforce the take-home messages through repetition.
  - Provide managers with questions to ask staff to spur discussion.

- Developing large- and small-scale training sessions.
  - Introduction and kick-off of service recovery lends itself to large-scale sessions, which generate energy and excitement.
  - Feature the best in your staff members in your formal training.
  - Go to department staff meetings for 10–15 minute trainings. Make them interactive.
  - Keep small-scale sessions to an hour of less. Anything longer will make people tired and, often, forgetful. Make them multidisciplinary. Bring together people

from diverse areas of your organization to draw them out of their comfort zone, create new connections, and subtly emphasize the message that this is an organization-wide initiative, not just nurses or one department. Spend most of the session practicing in small groups of two or three.

- Developing a support packet or "toolkit" for managers and front-line staff. (Sample toolkits are contained in the CD that accompanies this book.) A toolkit should include materials that reinforce what was taught in training.

- Taking advantage of e-learning technologies for interactive training modules. For example, Advocate Healthcare (Oak Brook, IL) uses a game show theme to illustrate the concepts of service recovery and convey their message to staff. The idea is to inform people that complaints are gifts that give you the opportunity to improve patient care. (Sample training games are contained in the CD that accompanies this book).

- Making certain that participants evaluate the quality of each session. Test later to ensure that learning has occurred.

Many of these best practices are described in greater detail later, but this overview gives you an idea of the comprehensive nature of your training initiative. Don't just pick one or two of the above, use them all.

Another progressive health system we worked with provides an outstanding example of integrating all of these best practices with a foundation training for these skills. First, associates are only hired if they demonstrate an aptitude for service excellence and live one of the organization's most important values: *compassion.* All staff undergo rigorous customer service training, service recovery training, and empathetic communication skills training. Training is ongoing to ensure continued understanding and a degree of uniformity. A service recovery fund exists for any staff to use at their discretion (e.g., to make amends for service failure or to exceed the expectations of patients). For a growing number of healthcare organizations, excellence in customer service is an absolute fundamental.

Basic customer service training

Memorial Hospital Pembroke (FL) has six classes that all staff must attend when they join the organization:

Class one: First impressions
A video of do's and don'ts
"You only have one chance to make a first impression"
Disney's approach to impressing the customer
Why first impressions are lasting
Dressing for success

Class two: Achieving excellence
Successful customer service organizations—what makes them that way?
What makes customer service in healthcare different?
The benefits of customer service
How to get from where we are to where we want to be—and stay there
Begin with the end in mind

Class three: Customer service principles
Basic rules of customer service
Reasons why patients recommend hospitals
Five key concepts of customer service
The importance of word-of-mouth

Class four: Teamwork
Building a strong sense of teamwork
Working as part of a customer service team
Defining the essential skills needed to provide wow service
Interdepartmental cooperation

Class five: Effective communication
Verbal and nonverbal communication
Telephone etiquette
Active listening skills
Demonstrate to customers that what they have to say is important to you:

- ✔ Focus on the customer's needs
- ✔ Avoid interrupting when the customer speaks
- ✔ Verify and clarify what the customer is saying
- ✔ Maintain eye contact
- ✔ Ask questions in organized sequence

Class six: Resolving customer problems
Identify reasons for customer problems
Why healthcare is a problem-prone business

- ✔ Problems are the nature of our business (patients and families come to us in an already high state of stress, the family's expectation of care is higher than the patient's, and we deal in highly complicated, confusing systems)
- ✔ Expectations of care continue to grow
- ✔ Increased public attention to healthcare (puts us in spotlight)

The common problems and how to resolve them
The best way to avoid problems
What customers want most and get the least

TRAINING CAMP

Floyd Medical Center (Rome, GA) takes a unique approach to their training program through the use of Camp FMC, an innovative four-day customer service training program in which all workers participate in a service recovery session.

The program starts with an explanation of why customer complaints are a good thing, how communication styles affect customer actions when a complaint comes up, and personal ways to deal with tense situations. Next, campers discover why service recovery is done and what its benefits are to the organization, the customer, and the staff. Actual cases from Floyd Medical Center files are used to measure the campers' understanding of the process. Campers are rewarded with "camp bucks" for appropriate service recoveries. During Camp FMC Talent Night, campers are given real scenarios of poor service to customers. Campers then write and act the correct way to handle the situations using their new skills learned at camp. As a result of Camp FMC training, the number of staff using service recovery has increased significantly. (See the CD for further information on Camp FMC.)

PRINTED HANDBOOKS AND MANUALS

Printed materials such as handbooks or manuals can be used to educate and train staff. Henry Ford Wyandotte Hospital uses a handbook to define its vision of service recovery, why it is important, and what role staff play in the process. They have built in the program's acronym by developing a STAR character named Howie Care. Howie may be cute, but he has an important message to convey, and he does it in a clear and concise manner.

Similarly, Western Maryland Health Systems prioritizes consistency in its service recovery approach. They make sure that each unit and department receives a service recovery manual that outlines the programs and materials available to all employees and taught to all employees at educational sessions (see the CD for a complete pdf of the manual).

COMPUTER-BASED TRAINING

Computers have become an integral tool for communication. Presentation software can be used to create slide shows, and the slides can be printed as handouts so participants can follow along and make notes. Photos can be placed on slides for added interest (see the CD for examples of these presentations).

A facility intranet allows you to share information within a secure environment. This network can only be accessed by the organization's members, employees, or others that have been given the authorization to access it. Announcements and updates can be posted as they occur and shared with others in the facility, as can handbooks, manuals, and forms. This system keeps everyone current about the service recovery program. Search capabilities add to the value of your facility's intranet as well.

Play 'The Service Is Right'

Advocate Health Care introduced a computer-based training module entitled "The Service Is Right" to build awareness of its service recovery process. The thirty-minute module helps staff understand what a complaint is, whether it is stated directly or indirectly, or whether it is overheard. The module teaches the actual steps of the process and emphasizes that the success of the program depends on following each step. An important piece of the module allows for practice by asking participants to choose what they might say or do in a specific situation and how they might say it to have the most positive effect (see the CD for the example).

Play 'Customer Service Feud'

Associates at St. Luke's enjoy playing the "Customer Service Feud" game that is used as a training tool. Computer screens flash questions geared toward service recovery, and associates are then asked to give their answers. The next screen displays the answers to the questions so associates can check their answers and discuss them.

Create a Theme Song

For the musically inclined, service recovery training can include song. Emory Hospital (Atlanta, GA) Environmental Services and Facilities' service recovery program penned a theme song to the tune of "Beautiful Dreamer." You probably won't hear it over your car radio, but it is clever just the same.

Beautiful Dreamer awake now and see/Hey you there sleeping in chair number three.

I know it's boring, but you've got to see/Just how important great service can be.

Beautiful Dreamer arise and go see/Just how happy your patients can be.

It's so amazing the change that occurs/When we treat our patients like our family.

MAKE A VIDEO

Lights, camera, action! You can gather all the budding actors and actresses in your facility to help with service recovery training. Clever skits can be videotaped and shown at new-hire orientations, specific training sessions, or any other appropriate venue. People can be extremely creative when writing and performing, and they also can really get the point across. People also enjoy seeing coworkers as actors—and what a way to create ownership in a program.

Sample videos

Russell Medical Center (Alexander City, AL) made the video "Mrs. Worth-a-lot gets the Runaround" to show during its initial rollout and then presented it during each new employee orientation session. In the video, poor Mrs. Worth-a-lot tries to find her way to the business office of a busy hospital. While wandering through the hall, she encounters some interesting, but not very helpful, characters.

Addy Tude is too busy on her personal phone call to escort Mrs. Worth-a-lot and instead just barks out detailed directions at a rapid pace. Nosey Rosie and Miss Bee Havior can't be bothered to help because their attention is focused on their personal conversation. It isn't until Mrs. Worth-a-lot finally meets Mr. Caramore Harris that she can fulfill her mission. Even though she tells him that she feels like a world traveler after her long and lonely trip through the hospital, he responds to her needs using the service recovery CARE components of connect, apologize, resolve, and evaluate. Only after being treated with sincerity, respect, and compassion is Mrs. Worth-a-lot able to donate that big bag of money to the hospital (see the DVD for more videos).

Holzer Medical Center (Gallipolis, OH) created a video to demonstrate scenarios that had gone awry and to teach their associates how to fix the problem and the process itself. The different departments viewed it and discussed the scenes. The scenarios were all things that could happen at any facility, but they need to be addressed. For example, a scene portraying an argumentative staff member illustrates the need to learn to listen. The patient did not want to hear the staff member say, "Don't worry about it, honey." Or a scene where an obviously ill patient is wheeled, coughing and sneezing, next to another patient illustrated the need to see yourself in the patient's shoes. Service recovery is necessary to reassure the patient that the unwelcome guest did not have tuberculosis or "who-knows-what-kind of germs."

Women & Infants Hospital's (Providence, RI) video drives home the fact that service issues cannot always be prevented but that the way in which staff handle the situation can turn a negative experience into a positive experience. In one scene, a patient asks for someone who can offer assistance and provide information. Getting the answer, "Good luck finding anyone who knows anything," from a staff member does not help the patient have a good experience. With the proper training, however, this situation can be turned around.

The DVD that accompanies this book provides more examples of service recovery videos.

Create a toolkit

The best builder in the world cannot work without the proper tools. When building a service recovery program, staff members need to be given the tools to complete the task at hand. Toolkits enable staff members to make amends quickly.

One goal of an effective service recovery program is to make participation desirable for all staff members and to make using the toolkit convenient. The apology cards, forms, gifts, and other elements of the program should be grouped together, centrally located, and easy to access. Often, several of the toolkits are located throughout the facility in each unit or department and can be replenished by a quick message to the service recovery team. Other facilities may have a central location for the toolkit.

The cost of a toolkit in your program may vary from a few hundred dollars to nearly one thousand dollars a month. In many situations, it may be sufficient to let the patient know that someone is listening by giving a sincere apology and presenting the patient with a name and phone number to contact should any further issues arise.

Programs may have different levels of complaint severity, and the value of the items in the toolkits increases as the severity level increases. In minor recovery situations, an apology card, which is part of the toolkit, is sufficient. Higher severity recoveries may involve the offer of a gift card, vending machine or cafeteria vouchers, parking vouchers, fruit baskets, candy, or flowers as an apology or method of atonement for the patient's inconvenience. Some organizations use an item that is unique to their area, such as Vermont maple syrup, for special gifts. Doing so also allows them to support and advertise local businesses.

Keep stocks of the gift cards in the toolkit. Toolkits may even contain vouchers for a free service such as a massage. Staff members should be encouraged to make the gift appropriate to the situation (e.g., gas cards or taxi vouchers for cancelled appointments or cafeteria certificates for food delivered late or cold).

Toolkits also should contain some form of tracking system. A two-part form with a bottom part that can be turned in to a central department works well. That way, the individual with overall responsibility for the service recovery program can make sure that the toolkits are replenished when contents are running low. (Sample tracking forms are included in the CD.)

There are many items that can be put into your toolkit. Below is a brief list of some toolkit items (see the CD for further examples):

- Apology card
- Taxi or parking vouchers
- Movie tickets
- Food vouchers
- Flowers
- Gift baskets
- Gift certificates
- Toys, puzzles, and small stuffed animals

Toolkits also can contain scripts to follow when going through the service recovery process, which helps maintain consistency in how recoveries are handled and helps to make sure all the appropriate steps in the program are followed.

Lexington Medical Center's toolkit

Lexington Medical Center uses its GIFT theme for its toolkit. Any employee involved in the resolution of a patient/family complaint or concern may obtain a gift as an additional way to offer an apology. The gift serves as an indicator for staff that this patient/family member has already had a negative experience and so should be given special attention. Gifts may be obtained from designated locations in departments or in the Guest Services office, bought from the hospital gift shop, or paid for out of a special fund to purchase additional items. The average monthly bill from the gift shop was approximately $600 for thirty or so gifts.

Sharp Metropolitan Medical Campus' toolkit

A service recovery toolkit is available for Sharp Metropolitan Medical Campus managers to pick up and place on their unit. It is maintained through the Patient Relations department, which receives the tracking forms that are filled out when a staff member uses a tool, and these items could be parking passes, food vouchers, or gift certificates to coffee carts or the gift shop. The Patient Relations department replenishes the toolkit to maintain par levels using the tracking forms. All staff members have access to a toolkit on all shifts. It is as simple as having plastic file folders that house parking vouchers, food vouchers, Starbucks gift cards, or gift shop certificates. Instructions for using the toolkit are on the front of the folder. Staff members are encouraged to use their best judgment in picking an item that best fits the situation, and are encouraged to ask a supervisor if they are uncertain as to which item to use. Managers are expected to acknowledge and reward staff members who use the toolkit items.

Sharp classified its tools into three levels based on the severity of the service failure. Mild service failures could receive a parking coupon, a $3 or $5 food coupon, or candy. Moderate service failures might be made right by parking coupons, $6 food coupons, $10 or $25 gift shop coupons, movie tickets, or flowers. Severe failures mean staff should contact their manager.

Henry Ford Wyandotte's toolkit

Henry Ford Wyandotte teaches its staff that customers are more interested in getting things resolved, receiving a sincere apology, and ensuring that it doesn't happen to others than they are in receiving a token gift. However, if any staff member feels that more than an apology is necessary, gifts are available in the department's "treasure chest" to enhance the apology. Gifts are not meant to fix the problem; they are meant to help compensate for an inconvenience or unnecessary expense to the customer. Staff members use their own judgment regarding situations when a sincere apology is enough and a gift is not appropriate. When items from the treasure chest are used, they are appropriate to the situation.

Waukesha Memorial Hospital's toolkit

Waukesha Memorial Hospital (Waukesha, WI) made a commitment to providing employees with the tools to recover from service breakdowns. The process included a service recovery toolkit that was piloted in six areas of the hospital (ED, admitting, surgical inpatient unit, women's health, breast center, and admitting nurse supervisors). Contents of the kit included movie tickets, apology notes, gift certificates, and other recovery items, as needed. If the contents of the toolkit do not meet the employees' needs, they can contact the Customer Relations department for further recovery tools.

Hospital staff in service recovery training also will appreciate receiving small gifts to show appreciation for their time and effort. "Training take-aways" of binders, bookmarks, certificates, or mugs or pens with your facility's logo make great gift ideas.

Provide scripting

Words are powerful. Anyone who has been on the receiving end of harsh words knows how unkind words can wound. Scripting is a powerful tool that uses words and behaviors to "convey clear, consistent, and caring messages . . . to build trust between the staff and the patient, family member, and visitors."[1] Press Ganey's research has shown that staff interaction with patients and family members is highly correlated to patients' overall satisfaction with their inpatient experience. Most organizations understand the impact of staff/patient interactions and also recognize that the difficulty lies not in understanding the concept of scripting but in knowing how to implement scripts in a way that creates a trusting relationship.

Scripting does not just mean the verbatim spoken word. It can also include a "directorial" component that guides the actor to do such things as the following:

- Knocking before entering rooms.
- Smiling and making eye contact.
- Greeting the patient by name.
- Introducing yourself and saying what your role is and what you are going to do.

Staff members should be taught to empathize with patients, and scripting is a great aid when dealing with problem situations. Tell patients that you want to provide them with very good care. For those times when an apology is needed, tell them you are very sorry that their expectations were not met. Teach that there is a right way and a wrong way to respond to situations. Training materials for scripting should be disseminated to all employees, with supervisors setting the example by using scripts of words and actions. Figure 8.1 provides some examples of what to say and what not to say. Additional scripts and training are contained in the CD that accompanies this book.

Figure 8.1

Baptist Hospital scripts

Don't say	*Say*
It's not my job.	Let me find someone who can help.
We've always done it this way.	Perhaps we could look at it from a new perspective.
How are we feeling today?	How are you feeling today?
Here we go again (when taking a complaint).	What can I do to help you?
Seen better days, haven't you?	How are you?
Sally, please walk this way so I can take your blood pressure.	Ms. Jones, please walk this way so I can take your blood pressure.
She's not here. Can you call back in five minutes?	She's not in. Can I help you?
What's wrong with you?	What can I do for you?
You needed to call sooner.	I'm sorry that date and time are not available.
We're swamped. I have too much to do.	Volume is up, but that's good, it means we're needed.
I'm glad you're my last patient.	I'm glad you're my patient.

CREATE SCRIPTS BASED ON PATIENT SATISFACTION SURVEYS

Press Ganey survey questions are a great tool for scripting. Scripts can be written for questions taken right from your survey.

Staff attitude toward visitors

Scripting for the question relating to staff's attitude toward visitors starts with engaging the visitor and saying, "Do you have someone in the hospital?" or "We want to provide very good care, can we do anything for you?"

Nurses' attitudes toward requests

Nurses can use a script such as, "Good morning, I am [name]. I am the nurse leader on this unit. I want to assure you that we will do everything possible to exceed your expectations. But, I need your help. This is my pager number and my phone number [write on patient communication board]. Please call me the moment you see or find something that we can do better or let me know of an opportunity where we can exceed your expectations. Our goal is to provide you with very good care."

Nurses kept you informed

Keeping the patient informed can be achieved by saying, "I am [name]. I will be your nurse until [time]. Please let me know the moment we can do something for you or do something better. My goal is to exceed your expectations and provide you with very good care."

Staff concern for your privacy

It is every staff member's responsibility to respect patient privacy. Every time a nurse or technician pulls a curtain around a bed or cubicle or closes a door, they say, "I am closing this door or pulling this curtain because I am concerned about your privacy."

Overall cheerfulness of the hospital

The simple act of saying to a patient before you leave his or her room, "Is there anything else that I can do for you? I certainly have time to help you," makes a huge contribution to the perception of overall cheerfulness of the hospital.

Staff addressed your emotional needs

Hospitalization is an emotional experience for patients, so it is important to treat the "whole person." Hospital staff should pay attention to the changing mental and emotional needs of patients by acknowledging that they are important. Try saying, "Being in the hospital can be tough emotionally and spiritually. We have chaplains (or social workers or counselors) in the hospital around the clock if you would like to talk. Would you like me to contact a chaplain (social worker, counselor) for you?"

Response to concerns or complaints

If your patients say, "I'm sorry to bother you," it may be because you've been treating them like an interruption. Change this by saying, "Of course you're not a bother . . ." Being more receptive when a patient says, "Oh, just one more thing," is accomplished by taking your hand off the door and listening attentively.

Staff sensitivity to inconvenience

Sometimes hospitalization is unexpected and the patient didn't have time to take care of things while away from home. Use scripting such as, "I realize that being admitted today was not something you expected to happen. Is there something we can do to make things go more smoothly at home?" Let the patient know you understand by saying, "I realize that being away from home is inconvenient. Is there something I can do to help, such as making a call for you? Do you need a phone, pen, or paper?"

Staff concern for your comfort during tests and treatments

Tests and treatments may seem like everyday duties to hospital staff, but it may be an uncomfortable time for patients. It makes all the difference when staff members express concern by saying, "For your comfort, I am giving you this warm blanket. Would you like some ice chips, juice, or soda? You will be more comfortable if you sip slowly." Staff should tell the family, "We want to make (Mr., Mrs., or Ms. and the last name of the patient) as comfortable as possible. Please let us know if you observe that (Mr., Mrs., or Ms. and the last name of the patient) is uncomfortable in any way."

Explanations of tests and treatment

When patients know the reason behind a process, they are more likely to cooperate. Support your patients when they ask a question by saying things like, "I'm glad you asked that." The more they ask, the more knowledgeable they will be.

Staff worked together for you

Patients perceive a facility that works together as a facility that works better. Try saying, "My shift will end in the next few minutes. The nurse for the next (number) hours will be (name), who will be here shortly. Is there anything else I can do for you?" In this way, there is not a break in the patient's care, and the patient feels more secure. Even the classic, "May I help you?" shows that every member of the staff is working as one to care for patients.

Scripting is about a facility adhering to the same standard operating procedure. Once everyone is saying and doing the same thing, you can move toward systematic and continuous quality improvement because you will have established a baseline.

Figure 8.2

Empathetic communication

Empathetic questions

What does all this mean to you?
Does anything worry you?
What is your biggest concern?
What questions do you have?
Would you like to add anything?
(Patient has brought a book) What are you reading? Tell me about it.
Avoid closed-ended questions such as, You don't really mean ___, do you?

Empathetic body language

Get on the patient's level—two minutes sitting by a patient's bed is better than ten minutes standing at the foot of the bed or fifteen minutes standing in the doorway with one's hand on the doorknob.
Lean toward the person.
Maintain eye contact.
Ask questions.
Use facial expressions, nod.

Empathetic responses

We're glad you're here. We're glad you're with us.
I sense that you are suffering/angry/sad/etc.
Thank you for sharing that with me.
It's not easy to be in the hospital.
It's difficult being away from those we love.
Anyone would be under stress in these circumstances.
It's ok to be worried. Your concerns are important to me too.
That's true.
Please, start at the beginning
Tell me more.
Can you add anything?
Can you give me an example?
What does that mean to you?
I see.
I'm listening.

Reflect content

Summarize the patient's major points.
Pause between sentences.
So you feel that…
From what I'm hearing you want…
It seems like you may be feeling ___. Is that how you are feeling? It's ok to be ___.
Let me be sure I understand your perspective.
I hear you saying…
Is this what you mean?
Let me see whether I follow you.
As I understand it…
Please correct me if I'm wrong, but what I hear you saying is _______.
I get the feeling that ___. Is that the way you see it?
Let's see if I understood you. You said…
Am I on target with what you meant?

Figure 8.3

Non-empathetic communication

Lecturing

Judging
You thought what?
How could you?
Why didn't you . . . ?
Don't you know that . . . ?

Negative responses
It must be humiliating to have this disease.
I can't imagine how you can go on living with this.

Advising
You should . . .
Have you considered . . . ?

Interpreting
Of course you're having difficulty. You've got a . . .

Cliches
Remember, Rome wasn't built in a day.
Love conquers all.

Psychoanalyzing
Your anxiety about this procedure suggests to me you're confused about sexuality.

Philosophizing and mystifying
You're an Aquarius. That means you can expect to get depressed from time to time.
You're struggling with Dark Forces. Accept your inner light.

Sincere non-empathy

Sympathy
I know how bad it is to be recovering from a car accident. I broke my leg in a car accident.

Pitying or humoring
That must hurt so bad. I feel sorry for you.
You poor thing.

Interrogating or interviewing
You couldn't sleep last night? How often do you lose sleep? Did you not sleep the entire night? Are you sure it wasn't something you ate? I know that when I eat something spicy it will keep me up all night!

Denying feeling
Don't worry. You'll be home soon. It will all get better.
Your problem isn't so bad. Look at all the troubles your roommate is having.
At least you made it out of the accident alive.

Inappropriately sharing personal feelings (ignoring the other person's feelings)
Patient: The stoma nurse came and showed me how to clean this, but I don't know how I can live like this. It's so strange, unnatural. I'm afraid people will find out.
Listener: I want you to know that I care for you and your emotional needs.

Figure 8.3

Non-empathetic communication (cont.)

Near empathy	Words that wound
Missing the point while saying something generally true: Patient: This isn't supposed to be happening to me. Not at this age. Listener: It's not unusual to feel frustrated. Frustration can lead to anger. *Narrowly focusing on a minor or irrelevant point* Okay. So you can't do the things you really love anymore, but isn't it nice to be retired? You say you're worried about whether your son in the Army will get to see you, but at least we live in a great, safe country thanks to people like him. *Repeating the obvious (parroting)* Patient: This surgery makes me nervous. Listener: You feel nervous. Patient: I didn't tell my daughter about this. She doesn't know I'm in the hospital. Now, I'm worried because what if something happens to me? Listener: So, you're worried something might happen to you. *Getting the wrong hidden feeling* Patient: I don't have anyone to talk to. When I go home, nobody visits me, nobody calls, nobody cares. Listener: The world is treating you bad and you feel like you need to get even. *Being vague and imprecise* You're feeling old. Sounds like you're sort of sad or angry. Any cancer diagnosis is a concern, so that's why you called life 'hopeless' and 'bleak'. You're feeling down. *Professing understanding when one doesn't understand* Yes! Yes! I know exactly what you're talking about! Oh, I completely understand.	I don't have time to look for your lost _______. Our lost-and-found that handles that. Call this number. Maybe it will turn up. That's not our policy. I'm new here, so I don't really know about that. We're just so busy right now and very short staffed. They never get anything right.

Reward and recognize

The intrinsic value of making a moment in life better for someone is probably the best reward and recognition that anyone can ever get, and that is why many people choose healthcare as their profession. Nonetheless, it is also nice to be recognized by a boss or a coworker.

Rewarding and recognizing specific behaviors and results improves performance through positive reinforcement. It is simply one of many strategies proven to create an environment conducive to achieving desired results. It is vital to reward and recognize employees committed to service recovery.

FREE MEALS

Lexington Medical Center holds a contest in which every employee using the service recovery process receives a free meal in the cafeteria for every time they use the program. This includes ancillary departments such as physical therapy, engineering, and nutrition services. At the end of the allotted time, the department with the most usage (based on bed capacity) receives a gift for their department, and in addition to the gift, one person's name is drawn for eight hours of paid time off.

Pick up a copy of the service recovery handbook at Henry Ford Wyandotte Hospital and you will see multiple items communicating the importance of reward and recognition listed in the talking points and tips for managers (see the CD for more information). Employees will benefit from feedback on their involvement in service recovery.

FREE POPCORN

Simple though it sounds, it works. Waukesha Memorial Hospital put a step into their process so that when employees submit complaint tracking forms, they receive a coupon for free popcorn in the employee cafeteria. (An example of this coupon is contained in the CD that accompanies this book.)

PUBLISH THE NAMES OF SERVICE RECOVERY STARS

Sharp Metropolitan Medical Campus publishes their newsletter "We've Got the Point!" Not only can you find facts and examples of service recovery, you also will find a listing of employees who are being recognized with, "Congratulations to all of you who are making it better and practicing service recovery! Kudos to those listed below who are using the toolkit!"

Track and trend

Service recovery programs are put in place to help focus the organization in meeting their customer-service excellence goals. To do that, tracking how and where service recovery efforts occur and looking at trends make it possible to avoid subsequent service failure.

SIGN IN TO A LOG

When a service recovery opportunity occurs at Lexington Medical Center, the staff member handling the situation simply signs in to a log and provides details of the service problem and what was done to respond to it. The service recovery log is monitored every month to provide trending information about processes or systems that need to be improved. Frequently, an ad hoc team is put together to address the issues. New scripting might be developed, or a more efficient way to do a task might be found. Each department receives a report on all patient complaints and a report on all service recovery opportunities. Using the trending data, processes are put into place to recognize the potential for lapses in service. Every department can identify "automatic service recovery opportunities."

ENTER THE COMPLAINT WITHIN ONE DAY

Southern Ohio Medical Center enters complaints into the complaint management software system within one business day. A complaint report and resolution form is generated and sent to the appropriate department manager or physician director. The department manager or physician director investigates the complaint and responds within seven days. A summary report is sent to department managers monthly for review analysis and action to improve. Total complaints per fiscal year are graphically represented to watch trends.

THE TRACKING FORM

A key to a successful service recovery program is using a tracking form that has space to gather the who, what, and why of the service recovery action. Staff at the facility can use a two-part tracking form to record the information. Part of the form is given to the customer to be redeemed, and the other part is used for tracking and trending. These forms can be put into the toolboxes or at a central location. An example of a multi-part certificate is used at Scott & White Hospital (Temple, TX). Examples of forms can be found in the CD.

Conclusion

If imitation is the most sincere form of flattery, taking something from the examples we have presented here is great praise for the facilities that shared their experiences. Your service recovery program will be as unique as your facility, but these ideas will be a great jumping-off place.

Sometimes we focus a little too much on the serious nature of the physical health issues at stake in healthcare. We forget about the *care*. We're here to give of ourselves and *care* for those less fortunate, beset by illness, or struggling to live a better life. We all want them to *feel* how much we *care*. To experience soul-refreshing, heart-mending, and inspirational care creates an emotional bond between everyone. Together, let's create a universal environment for healthcare that cures and inspires everyone—patients, residents, employees, and physicians.

Endnote

1. Jackie Ryan and Sharyl Wojciechowski, "More than Words, RX for Scripting Challenges: Best Practices Techniques," *The Satisfaction Monitor* (July/August 2003).

Part V

Appendices

Appendix A

Centers for Medicaid & Medicare Services Conditions of Participation Interpretative Guidelines

A-0041

§482.13(a)(2) The hospital must establish a process for prompt resolution of patient grievances and must inform each patient whom to contact to file a grievance.

Interpretive guidelines §482.13(a)(2)

The patient should have reasonable expectations of care and services and the facility should address those expectations in a timely, reasonable, and consistent manner. Although §482.13(a)(2)(ii) and (iii) address documentation of facility time frames for a response to a grievance, the expectation is that the facility will have a process to comply with a relatively minor request in a more timely manner than a written response. For example, a change in bedding, housekeeping of a room, and serving preferred food and beverages may be made relatively quickly and would not usually be considered a "grievance" and therefore would not require a written response.

The hospital must inform the patient and/or the patient's representative of the internal grievance process, including whom to contact to file a grievance (complaint). As part of its notification of patient rights, the hospital must provide the patient or the patient's representative a phone number and address for lodging a grievance with the State agency.

The hospital must inform the patient that he/she may lodge a grievance with the State agency (the State agency that has licensure survey responsibility for the hospital) directly, regardless of whether he/she has first used the hospital's grievance process.

*A **"patient grievance"** is a written or verbal complaint (when the verbal complaint about patient care is not resolved at the time of the complaint by staff present) by a patient, or the patient's representative, regarding the patient's care, abuse or neglect, issues related to the hospital's compliance* *with the CMS Hospital Conditions of Participation (CoP), or a Medicare beneficiary billing complaint related to rights and limitations provided by 42 CFR §489.*

- ***"Staff present"*** *includes any hospital staff present at the time of the complaint or who can quickly be at the patient's location (i.e. nursing, administration, nursing supervisors, patient advocates, etc.) to resolve the patient's complaint.*

- *If a verbal patient care complaint cannot be resolved at the time of the complaint by staff present, is postponed for later resolution, is referred to other staff for later resolution, requires investigation, and/or requires further actions for resolution, then the complaint is a grievance for the purposes of these requirements. A complaint is considered resolved when the patient is satisfied with the actions taken on their behalf.*

- *Billing issues are not usually considered grievances for the purposes of these requirements. However, a Medicare beneficiary billing complaint related to rights and limitations provided by 42 CFR §489 are considered a grievance.*

- *A written complaint is always considered a grievance, whether from an inpatient, outpatient, released/discharged patient or their representative regarding the patient care provided, abuse or neglect, or the hospital's compliance with CoPs. For the purposes of this requirement an e-mail or fax is considered "written."*

- *Information obtained with patient satisfaction surveys does not usually meet the definition of a grievance. If an identified patient writes or attaches a written complaint on the survey and requests resolution, then the complaint meets the definition of a grievance. If an identified patient writes or attaches a complaint to the survey but has not requested resolution, the hospital must treat this as a grievance if the hospital would usually treat such a complaint as a grievance.*

- *Patient complaints that become grievances also include situations where a patient or a patient's representative telephones the hospital with a complaint regarding their patient care or with an allegation of abuse or neglect, or failure of the hospital to comply with one or more CoPs, or other CMS requirements. Those post-hospital verbal communications regarding patient care that would routinely have been handled by staff present if the communication had occurred during the stay/visit are not required to be defined as a grievance.*

- *All verbal or written complaints regarding abuse, neglect, patient harm, or hospital compliance with CMS requirements, are to be considered a grievance for the purposes of these requirements.*

- *Whenever the patient or the patient's representative requests their complaint be handled as a formal complaint or grievance or when the patient requests a response from the hospital, then the complaint is a grievance and all the requirements apply.*

- *Data collected regarding patient grievances, as well as some other complaints that are not defined as grievances (as determined by the hospital) must be incorporated in the hospital's Quality Assessment and Performance Improvement Program (QAPI).*

SURVEY PROCEDURES §482.13(A)(2)

- Review the hospital's policies and procedures to assure that its grievance process encourages all personnel to alert appropriate staff concerning any patient grievance. Does the hospital adhere to its policy/procedure established for referrals?

- Interview patients or the patient's legal representative to determine if they know how to file a complaint (grievance) and who to contact if they have a complaint (grievance).

- Is the hospital following its grievance policies and procedures?

- Does the hospital's process assure that grievances involving situations or practices that place the patient in immediate danger are resolved in a timely manner?

- Does the patient or the patient's representative know that he/she has the right to file a complaint with the State agency as well as or instead of utilizing the hospital's grievance process?

- Has the hospital provided the telephone number for the State agency to all patients/patient representatives?

- Are beneficiaries aware of their right to seek review by the Quality Improvement Organization (QIO) for quality of care issues, coverage decisions, and to appeal a premature discharge?

The hospital's governing body must approve and be responsible for the effective operation of the grievance process, and must review and resolve grievances, unless it delegates the responsibility in writing to a grievance committee.

Interpretive Guidelines §482.13(a)(2)

The hospital's grievance process must be approved by its governing body. The hospital's governing body is responsible for the effective operation of the grievance process, which includes the hospital's compliance with all the CMS grievance process requirements. The hospital's governing body must review and resolve grievances, unless it delegates this responsibility in writing to a grievance committee. A committee is more than one person. The committee membership must have adequate numbers of qualified members to review and resolve the grievances the hospital receives (this includes providing written responses) in a manner that complies with the CMS grievance process requirements.

Survey Procedures §482.13(a)(2)

- Determine if the hospital's governing body approved the grievance process?
- Is the governing body responsible for reviewing and resolving grievances, or has the governing body delegated the responsibility in writing to a grievance committee?
- Determine how effectively the grievance process works. Are patient's or the patient representative's concerns addressed in a timely manner? Are patients informed of any resolution to their grievances? Does the hospital apply what it learns from the grievance as part of its continuous quality improvement activities?
- Is the grievance process reviewed and analyzed through the hospital's QAPI process or other mechanism that provides oversight of the grievance process?

A-0043

The grievance process must include a mechanism for timely referral of patient concerns regarding quality of care or premature discharge to the appropriate Utilization and Quality Control, Quality Improvement Organization.

Interpretive Guidelines §482.13(a)(2)

Quality Improvement Organizations (QIO) are CMS contractors charged with reviewing the appropriateness and quality of care rendered to Medicare beneficiaries in the hospital setting. The QIOs are also tasked with reviewing utilization decisions. Part of this duty includes reviewing discontinuation of stay determinations based upon a beneficiary's request. The regulations state the functions of the QIOs in order to make Medicare beneficiaries aware of the fact that if they have a **complaint regarding quality of care,** disagree with a coverage decision, or they wish to appeal a premature discharge, they may contact the QIO to lodge a complaint. The hospital is required to have procedures for referring Medicare beneficiary concerns to the QIOs; additionally, CMS expects coordination between the grievance process and existing grievance referral procedures so that beneficiary complaints are handled timely and referred to the QIO at the beneficiary's request.

This regulation requires coordination between the hospital's existing mechanisms for utilization review notice and referral to QIOs for Medicare beneficiary concerns (See 42 CFR part 489.27). This requirement does not mandate that the hospital automatically refer each Medicare beneficiary's grievance to the QIO; however, the hospital must inform all beneficiaries of this right, and comply with his or her request if the beneficiary asks for QIO review.

Medicare patients have the right to appeal a premature discharge (see Interpretive Guidelines for §482.13(a)). Pursuant to 42 CFR §412.42(c)(3), a hospital must provide a hospital-issued notice of noncoverage (HINN) to any fee-for-service beneficiary that expresses dissatisfaction with an impending hospital discharge. MA organizations are required to provide enrollees with a notice of noncoverage, known as the Notice of Discharge and Medicare Appeal Rights (NODMAR), only when a beneficiary disagrees with the discharge decision or when the MA organization (or hospital, if the MA organization has delegated to it the authority to make the discharge decision) is not discharging the enrollee, but no longer intends to cover the inpatient stay.

Survey Procedures §482.13(a)(2)

- Review patient discharge materials. Is the hospital in compliance with 42 CFR §489.27?

- Does the hospital grievance process include a mechanism for timely referral of Medicare patient concerns to the QIO? What time frames are established?

- Interview Medicare patients. Are they aware of their right to appeal premature discharge?

A-0044

§482.13(a)(2)(i) The hospital must establish a clearly explained procedure for the submission of a patient's written or verbal grievance to the hospital.

Interpretive Guidelines §482.13(a)(2)(i)

The hospital's procedure for a patient or the patient's representative to submit written or verbal grievances must be clearly explained. The patient or patient's representative should be able to clearly understand the procedure.

Survey Procedures §482.13(a)(2)(i)

- Review the information provided to patients that explains the hospital's grievance procedures. Does it clearly explain how the patient is to submit either a verbal or written grievance?

- Interview patients or patient representatives. Does the patient, or (if he/she is incapacitated) his/her representative, know about the grievance process and how to submit a grievance?

A-0045

§482.13(a)(2)(ii) The grievance process must specify time frames for review of the grievance and the provision of a response.

Interpretive Guidelines §482.13(a)(2)(ii)

The hospital must review, investigate, and resolve each patient's grievance within a reasonable time frame. For example, grievances about situations that endanger the patient, such as neglect or abuse, should be reviewed immediately, given the seriousness of the allegations and the potential for harm to the patient(s). However, regardless of the nature of the grievance, the hospital should make sure that it is responding to the substance of each grievance while identifying, investigating, and resolving any deeper, systemic problems indicated by the grievance.

Occasionally a grievance is complicated and may require an extensive investigation. *We recognize that staff scheduling as well as fluctuations in the numbers and complexity of grievances can affect the timeframes for the provision of written responses.* On average, a timeframe of 7 days for the provision of the response would be considered appropriate. We do not require that *every* grievance be resolved during the specified timeframe although most should be resolved. The Code of Federal Regulations at 42 CFR §482.13(a)(2)(iii) specifies information the hospital must include in their response.

If the grievance will not be resolved, or if the investigation is not or will not be completed within 7 days, the hospital should inform the patient or the patient's representative that the hospital is still working to resolve the grievance and that the hospital will follow-up with a written response within a stated number of days in accordance with each hospital's grievance policy. The hospital must attempt to resolve all grievances as soon as possible.

Survey Procedures §482.13(a)(2)(ii)

What time frames are established to review and respond to patient grievances? Are these time frames clearly explained in the information provided to the patient that explains the hospital's grievance process? On average, for most months does the hospital provide a written response to most of its grievances within 7 days?

A-0046

§482.13(a)(2)(iii) In its resolution of the grievance, the hospital must provide the patient with written notice of its decision that contains the name of the hospital contact person, the steps taken on behalf of the patient to investigate the grievance, the results of the grievance process, and the date of completion.

Interpretive Guidelines §482.13(a)(2)(iii)

The written notice of the hospital's determination regarding the grievance must be communicated appropriately to the patient or the patient's representative in a language and manner the patient or the patient's representative understands.

The hospital may use additional tools to resolve a grievance, such as meeting with the patient and his family, or other methods it finds effective. The regulatory requirements for the grievance process are minimum standards, and do not inhibit the use of additional effective approaches in handling patient grievances. However, in all cases the hospital must provide a written notice (response) to each patient's grievance(s). The written response must contain the elements listed in this requirement.

When a patient communicates a grievance to the hospital via email the hospital may provide its response via e-mail pursuant to hospital policy. (Some hospitals have policies against communicating to patients over email.) If the patient requests a response via e-mail, the hospital may respond via e-mail. In these circumstances and when the e-mail response contains the information stated in this requirement, the e-mail meets the requirement for a written response. The hospital must maintain evidence of its compliance with these requirements.

A grievance is considered resolved when the patient is satisfied with the actions taken on their behalf.

There may be situations where the hospital has taken appropriate and reasonable actions on the patient's behalf in order to resolve the patient's grievance and the patient or the patient's representative remains unsatisfied with the hospital's actions. In these situations the hospital may consider the grievance closed for the purposes of these requirements. The hospital must maintain documentation of its efforts and demonstrate compliance with CMS requirements.

In its written response, the hospital is not required to include statements that could be used in a legal action against the hospital, but the hospital must provide adequate information to address each item stated in this requirement. The hospital is not required to provide an exhaustive explanation of every action the hospital has taken to investigate the grievance, resolve the grievance or other actions taken by the hospital.

Survey Procedures §482.13(a)(2)(iii)

Review the hospital's copies of written notices (responses) to patients. Are all patients provided a written *response*? Do the *written responses* comply with the requirements?

APPENDIX B

MALCOLM BALDRIGE NATIONAL QUALITY AWARD CRITERIA RELEVANT TO SATISFACTION AND SERVICE RECOVERY

1.1B. COMMUNICATION AND ORGANIZATIONAL PERFORMANCE

(1) How do senior leaders communicate with, empower, and motivate all employees throughout the organization?

> How do senior leaders encourage frank, two-way communication throughout the organization?
>
> How do senior leaders take an active role in employee reward and recognition to reinforce high performance and a customer and business focus?

(2) How do senior leaders create a focus on action to accomplish the organization's objectives, improve performance, and attain your VISION?

> How do senior leaders include a focus on creating and balancing value for customers and other stakeholders in their organizational performance expectations?

3.2. CUSTOMER RELATIONSHIPS AND SATISFACTION

Describe how your organization builds relationships to acquire, satisfy, and retain customers; to increase customer loyalty; and to develop new opportunities.

Describe also how your organization determines customer satisfaction.

Within your response, include answers to the following questions:

3.2A. CUSTOMER RELATIONSHIP BUILDING

(1) How do you build relationships to acquire customers, to meet and exceed their expectations, to increase loyalty and repeat business, and to gain positive referrals?

(2) How do your key access mechanisms enable customers to seek information, conduct business, and make complaints?

What are your key access mechanisms?

> How do you determine key customer contact requirements for each mode of customer access?
>
> How do you ensure that these contact requirements are deployed to all people and processes involved in the customer response chain?

(3) How do you manage customer complaints?

> How do you ensure that complaints are resolved effectively and promptly?
>
> How do you minimize customer dissatisfaction and loss of repeat business?
>
> How are complaints aggregated and analyzed for use in improvement throughout your organization and by your PARTNERS?

(4) How do you keep your approaches to building relationships and providing customer access current with business needs and directions?

3.2B. CUSTOMER SATISFACTION DETERMINATION

(1) How do you determine customer satisfaction and dissatisfaction?

> How do these determination methods differ among customer groups?
>
> How do you ensure that your measurements capture actionable information for use in exceeding your customers' expectations, securing their future business, and gaining positive referrals?

How do you use customer satisfaction and dissatisfaction information for improvement?

(2) How do you follow up with customers on products, services, and transaction quality to receive prompt and actionable feedback?

(3) How do you obtain and use information on your customers' satisfaction relative to their satisfaction with your competitors and/or industry BENCHMARKS?

(4) How do you keep your approaches to determining satisfaction current with business needs and directions?

4.1. MEASUREMENT, ANALYSIS, AND REVIEW OF ORGANIZATIONAL PERFORMANCE

Describe how your organization measures, analyzes, aligns, reviews, and improves its performance at all LEVELS and in all parts of your organization.

Within your response, include answers to the following questions:

4.1A. PERFORMANCE MEASUREMENT

(1) How do you select, collect, align, and integrate data and information for tracking daily operations and for tracking overall organizational performance, including progress relative to strategic objectives and action plans?

What are your key organizational performance measures?

How do you use these data and information to support organizational decision making and innovation?

(2) How do you select and ensure the effective use of key comparative data and information to support operational and strategic decision making and innovation?

(3) How do you keep your performance measurement system current with business needs and directions?

How do you ensure that your performance measurement system is sensitive to rapid or unexpected organizational or external changes?

6.0. PROCESS MANAGEMENT—HEALTHCARE PROCESS

How are patient expectations addressed and considered?

What are your key performance assessments and measures or indications of the healthcare process?

APPENDIX C

SAMPLE BROCHURE

Complaint/Grievance Procedure

1. **Complaint or Grievance Management Process.** BAMC's objective is to investigate and resolve complaints as they occur or within 30 days of a reported occurrence. **You will not be penalized for filing a complaint.**
2. Various terms used to identify the patient registering a complaint or a grievance within the scope of patient rights at BAMC are defined as:
   a. **Complaint.** A complaint is defined as an allegation or source of dissatisfaction expressed verbally or in writing by a BAMC patient, family member, guardian, surrogate decision-maker, significant other or authorized representative about care and/or services provided by staff and/or health care providers.
   b. **Complainant.** The person who makes the complaint is defined as a complainant.
   c. **Grievance.** A grievance is a written complaint to a department, point of service or the Patient Rights Specialist expressing dissatisfaction with the resolution of a complaint. Grievances are required to be written appeals to a department or service area resolution that is disputed by a grievant.
   d. **Grievant.** A grievant is the person who files the written appeal described in 2c.
3. **Filing a Complaint.** Anyone may file a complaint verbally or in writing at the point of care/service location with a Department Director or their designee and expect documentation of their concerns. Any complainant may request assistance for filing a complaint from the Patient Rights Specialist or designee.

   Filing a Privacy Right Complaint. If you believe your privacy rights have been violated, you may file a written complaint with BAMC's Privacy Officer or with the Department of Health and Human Services. Please see Notice of Privacy Practices for details.
4. The investigation and resolution process should not exceed **30 days for both written and verbal complaints.** If a complaint requires additional time due to extenuating circumstances and the input of all parties involved, a mutually agreeable completion date will be determined.

   Written complaints from a complainant or authorized representative receive a written response indicating the steps taken to address the concerns, the name and phone number of the complaint facilitator or mediator, and a completion date.

   Verbal complaints from a complainant or authorized representative are responded to in a variety of ways, including personal interactions, telephone calls, and career management meetings.
5. **Filing a Grievance.** A grievance may be filed by a complainant who disputes a complaint resolution regarding his/her care or patient rights. A grievance process is considered to be a written appeal filed within **30 business days** of receiving a complaint resolution that is not satisfactory.

   Any grievant who cannot submit a written grievance may request assistance from the Patient Rights Specialist.

   Grievances cannot be filed for obtaining compensation for malpractice; a timely notice of claim should be filed instead. Notices of Claim are referred to the Risk Management Department for review.

– 5 –

10. For patients asked by Bay Area Medical Center to participate in a research project: All patients asked to participate in a research project will be given a description of expected benefits, discomforts, and risks of participating. These patients will also be given a full explanation of the procedures that will be followed. If alternative services are available, these patients will also be given a description of these services. All patients asked to participate will be told that refusal to participate will not compromise their access to services. Consent forms will be signed by the person(s) providing information to the patient.
11. Every patient shall have the opportunity to participate to the fullest extent possible in planning for his or her care and treatment. Except in emergencies when the patient lacks decision-making capacity and the need for treatment is urgent, the patient is entitled to the opportunity to discuss and request information related to the specific procedures and/or treatments, risks involved, possible length of recuperation, and medically reasonable alternatives and accompanying risks and benefits.
12. Patients can expect information about pain and pain relief measures, as well as health professionals who will respond quickly to reports of pain and who will believe the patient's self-assessment of pain.
13. Any patient may refuse treatment to the extent permitted by law and shall be informed of the medical consequences of the refusal, other appropriate care and services that the hospital provides, (the option of) transfer to another facility or referral to another clinic.
14. Every patient will be asked if they have an Advance Directive. If the patient doesn't have an Advance Directive but would like further information, this will be provided.
15. The patient or the patient's legally authorized representative shall give prior informed consent for the patient's participation in any form of experimental treatment, drugs or involvement in research projects. A patient who declines to participate in research or experimentation is entitled to the most effective care that the hospital can otherwise provide.
16. Every patient has the right to emergency care and will receive treatment within the medical and legal capabilities of the hospital. The hospital will provide evaluation, service and/or referral as indicated by the urgency of the case or when requested by the patient. The patient may not be transferred to another facility without being given a full explanation for the transfer including the need for risks, benefits, and alternatives to such a transfer, without provisions being made for continuing care and without acceptance by the receiving institution.
17. Every patient shall be permitted to examine his or her hospital bill and receive an explanation of the bill regardless of source of payment and every patient shall receive, upon request, information relating to financial assistance available through the hospital.
18. Patients have the right to be free from restraints of any form that are not medically necessary or are used as a means of coercion, discipline, convenience, or retaliation by staff.
19. Patients who are being treated for mental illness, a developmental disability, alcohol abuse or drug abuse have additional rights guaranteed by law. Please ask for separate brochure if not provided.

– 2 –

APPENDIX D

COMPLAINT RATES REPORTED IN PEER-REVIEWED STUDIES

Reduced complaints from 2.6 per 1000 ED visits to 0.6 per 1000 ED visits—TA Mayer, FR Cates, MJ Mastorovich, and DL Royalty, "Emergency department patient satisfaction: Customer service training improves patient satisfaction and ratings of physician and nurse skill," *Journal of Healthcare Management* 43, no. 5 (September–October 1998): 441.

1.12 per 1000—VT Chande, MS Bhende, and HW Davis, "Pediatric emergency department complaints: a three-year analysis of sources and trends," *Annals of Emergency Medicine* 20, no. 9 (September 1991): 1014.

0.69 complaints per 1000 patient visits—K Anderson, D Allan, and P Finucane. "A 30-month study of patient complaints at a major Australian hospital," *Journal of Quality Clinical Practice* 21, no. 4 (December 2001): 109.

1.42 per 1000—K Anderson, D Allan, and P Finucane, "Complaints concerning the hospital care of elderly patients: a 12-month study of one hospital's experience," *Age Ageing* 29, no. 5 (2000): 409.

1.32 per 1000—DM Taylor, RS Wolfe, and PA Cameron, "Analysis of complaints lodged by patients attending Victorian hospitals, 1997-2001," *Medical Journal of Australia* 181, no. 1 (July 5, 2004): 31.

6.2 per 1000—PA Curka, PE Pepe, BS Zachariah, GD Gray, and C Matsumoto, "Incidence, source, and nature of complaints received in a large, urban emergency medical services system," *Academy of Emergency Medicine* 2, no. 6 (June 1995).

Example calculation:

x = # complaints

y = # of patients

x/y = complaint rate per patient

(x/y) • 1000 = complaint rate per 1000 patients

If you have 3,800 patients discharged in one month with seven complaints, your complaint rate is 1.84.

They can make this real-time by simply programming it into an Excel spreadsheet.

Appendix E

Customer Service Standards: Examples from High-Performers and Top Improvers

Centra Health

- Smile and introduce yourself and your role
- Greet patients and visitors with a smile and hello
- If a patient or visitor needs directions, walk them to their destination
- Hold doors open for patients, visitors, and coworkers
- Ask whether you can help answer any questions
- Knock and wait for a response before entering a patient's room
- Sit down and speak at patient's eye level
- Explain what is going to happen
- Update waiting patients every 15 minutes
- Keep patient information confidential
- Close curtains and doors during exams and procedures
- Apologize for mistakes

St. Vincent's

These serve as our road map and strong foundation. What can we do to wow our patients and visitors?

- Attitude
- Call lights/Prompt service
- Providing direction/Acknowledging the customer
- Telephone etiquette
- Customer wait time
- Facility appearance
- Privacy and confidentiality

Beebe Medical Center: Customer Service Standards

"We are caring people serving with compassion, integrity, and excellence"

Standard 1: Courtesy
Kind gestures, polite words . . . make people feel special.

- Acknowledge the patient by surname unless otherwise directed; use first names for coworkers and children, professional title when in the presence of patients/visitors (e.g., Dr., Rev., Nurse).

- Do not use terms of endearment such as honey or dear. Do not "talk down" to a patient or second-guess their knowledge level. Your words should not insult.

- Be polite; use please and thank you. Thank customers for choosing Beebe Medical Center.

- Make every effort to maintain a quiet environment. Noise annoys and shows lack of consideration for the patient.

Standard 2: Anticipate needs
You will often know what people want before they have to ask . . . ACT.

- Be assertively friendly; watch for nonverbal cues that someone needs assistance. Anticipate needs so that the customer does not have to ask.

- Escort the customer to their destination.

- Patient call lights are everyone's responsibility: Answer as soon as initiated and respond to requests within three minutes.

- When people are sick or worried, every minute is an hour. Respect the customer's time. Provide a comfortable atmosphere for those waiting, and educate them on what to expect. An acceptable wait time for scheduled appointments is 15 minutes. Keep customers informed of progress, and encourage them to bring extended waits to your attention.

- Manage patient expectations; be proactive. Use department scripts to answer frequently asked questions.

Standard 3: Attitude

The patient could be your child, your spouse, or your parent . . . choose your attitude.

- Present a caring, compassionate, and enthusiastic attitude. Assume full responsibility for presenting a positive attitude every day, every shift.

- Serve customers, exceed expectations

Standard 4: Confidentiality/Privacy

Watch what you say and do, where you say and do it . . . show respect.

- Adhere strictly to the confidentiality policy: Release information only to authorized persons; never discuss patient information in public areas; close curtains or doors during all exams and procedures.

- Provide a second gown of the right size for patients. Cover patients with blankets for comfort and modesty.

Standard 5: Listening and communicating

Slow down . . . give . . . imagine you are on the receiving end.

- Acknowledge a customer's presence immediately; introduce yourself by name and role; listen to customers; make eye contact; smile and be courteous.

- Use a pleasant, caring, and sincere tone of voice. Do not use jargon. Be aware of your environment and who is within hearing range.

- Give the customer all of your attention. Ask questions to clarify and validate what you think you have heard and understood.

- Never argue or challenge a customer. Watch for body language that may be conveying a negative message.

Standard 6: Professional image

You are part of a long, proud medical tradition . . . LOOK THE PART.

- Display "on stage" behaviors in all customer areas. Never show anger or frustration; don't gossip or discuss personal issues.

- Keep work area clean and orderly.

Standard 7: Safety

Care for our environment; it is our environment of caring.

- Support the "Our House" concept. It is everyone's responsibility to keep the facility safe and clean.

- Pick up litter and dispose of it properly. Block off spills, and clean them up promptly.

- Report all accident/incidents promptly; correct or report any safety hazards you see.

- Use protective clothing, gloves, and procedures when appropriate.

Standard 8: Service recovery

If a customer complains, do not be defensive; their perception is their reality.

Act to reverse a negative service situation by using the four A's:

- Anticipate: the needs, wants, expectations, and emotions of the customer to prevent dissatisfaction.

- Acknowledge: the customer's concerns—no excuses. Work to restore the complaint, not dismiss it. Take ownership; do not blame someone else or a department; avoid a defensive response; do not take the complaint personally; do not argue.

- Apologize: listen to the complaint; thank the customer for bringing it to your attention; summarize what you heard to confirm your understanding; apologize for the customer's negative experience as they have described it.

- Amend: offer suggestions for resolution; ask whether these suggestions will meet their expectations; ask if there is something else you can do for them; take whatever action is necessary to resolve the problem; ask others to help if necessary; inform the customer of your actions; offer a sincere token of apology.

Standard 9: Teamwork and commitment to BMC

Help each other and you help a patient.

- Treat one another as professionals deserving courtesy, honesty, and respect; cooperate with one another; do not undermine other people's work; do not chastise or embarrass fellow team members in the presence of others; avoid last-minute requests; offer to help whenever possible.

- Welcome newcomers; recognize one another; act as a teacher and role model to others.

- Take ownership of problems and take them to the appropriate supervisor; be prepared with possible solutions.

- Take pride in the organization as if you own it; accept the responsibilities of your job; adhere to all policies and procedures; live the values of Beebe Medical Center.

STANDARD 10: TELEPHONE AND ELEVATOR ETIQUETTE

When you greet a customer, our reputation is on the line; sound pleasant, be helpful, and listen with understanding.

- Know how to operate your phone. Answer calls by the third ring; answer with a smile, and use the universal greeting ("Good morning/afternoon/evening. BMC, department, this is . . . How may I help you?")

- Ask permission to place the caller on hold, to transfer, to give them voicemail, or to use a speakerphone. Transfer a caller only once; place them on hold for no longer than 30 seconds without acknowledgement.

- When entering or exiting an elevator, always smile and greet fellow passengers; hold doors open for others. Allow passengers to exit the elevator before getting on yourself.

- Patients and visitors always ride first. Always walk departing guests to the elevator.
- Face patients in wheelchairs toward the door. When transporting a patient on a stretcher or bed, ask others to take the next elevator. Speak to the patient and inform him or her of what to expect next.
- Do not discuss patient information, hospital business, or personal issues on the elevator.

WE COMMIT TO PROVIDE
VERY GOOD CARE and

Safety

s**E**nse of ownership

Respect

Stri**V**e to master skills

Image

Communication

T**E**amwork

Havasu Regional Medical Center

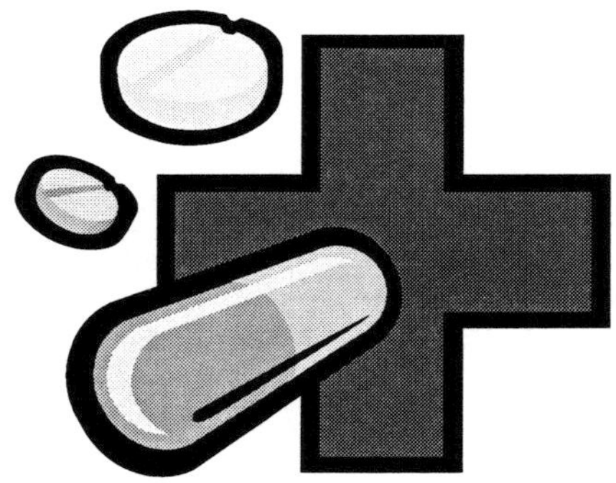

SAFETY AWARENESS:

Safety will be the responsibility of all Havasu Regional Medical Center employees to ensure an accident-free environment. “Think safe, act safe, be safe and stay safe.” That is a fundamental part of your job performance. Accidents are the result of actions and attitudes that you can help eliminate. Report all accidents and incidents promptly and completely.

- If you see a safety hazard, correct it if possible; report it if not.
- Do not take unnecessary chances.
- Know the policies and procedures, both hospital-wide and departmentally, relating to safety issues.
- Practice safety as a courtesy to your co-workers, your patients and all others.
- Protect your back when lifting, pushing, pulling or carrying. Get help when necessary.
- Be aware of potential chemical hazards; it is your right to know.
- Respect all machinery. Be sure it is in good working order and use it in the proper manner.
- Prevent slips, trips and falls.
- Be prepared for emergencies and know the correct and prompt actions to take.

If in doubt, ASK.

SENSE OF OWNERSHIP:

Every Havasu Regional Medical Center employee must feel a sense of ownership toward his or her job. By this we mean taking pride in what we do, feeling responsible for the outcomes of our efforts, and recognizing our work as a reflection of ourselves. Take pride in this organization as if you owned it.

- Be sure you know and understand the responsibilities of your job. Take charge and accept these responsibilities.
- Adhere to organization and departmental policies regarding tardiness, breaks and time clocks.
- Keep your work area and surrounding environment clean and safe.
- Strive to do the job right the first time. Focus on customers' needs.
- Look beyond your assigned tasks. Your responsibility does not end where your co-workers' responsibilities begin. In most situations, responsibilities merge and blend. When it is appropriate for you to perform a service, do so.
- Do not say, "It's not my job." If you are unable to meet a request, be responsible for finding someone who can.
- Perform your work in a timely manner. Meet customers' needs as soon as possible.
- Pay attention to details.
- Complete tasks. If interrupted, return to the job as soon as possible. If you are unable to finish a task, find someone who can.
- Conduct yourself as a professional. Help create a culture that taps the full potential of employees and builds an environment that allows all people to feel appreciated, included and valued.

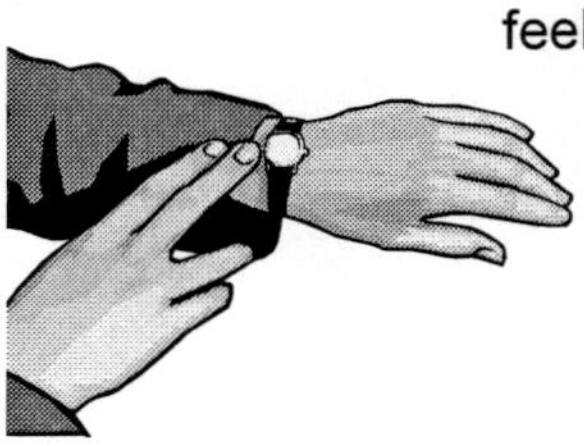

RESPECT:

At Havasu Regional Medical Center we believe that we are here to serve our customers. Our customers' most basic expectation is to be treated with courtesy and respect. This commitment must be reflected in our behavior. We are committed to providing the highest quality of service. We will treat our customers with the utmost care and courtesy. We will respect the privacy and confidentiality of the people we serve. We will ensure our customers' right to privacy and modesty by creating and maintaining a secure and trusting environment. When entrusted with a customers' affairs, we will treat all information as confidential. Discussion of these matters will be restricted to situations where the information is necessary to meet the customers' health needs. Our concern for our customers' privacy will help promote peace of mind and lessen their anxiety.

- Promptly welcome your customers in a friendly manner, smiling and introducing yourself. Don't allow anyone to feel ignored.
- Listen carefully to what your customers have to say. Avoid interrupting people unnecessarily.
- Treat everyone as if her or she is the most important person in our facility.
- Rudeness is never accepted.
- Meet the customer's immediate need or gladly take him or her to someone who will.
- Apologize for problems and inconveniences.
- Thank our customers for choosing our hospital.
- Exceed our customers' expectations.
- Recognize that our customers have a sense of urgency and show them that we value their time. Customers are not an interruption of our work; they are our reason for being here.

CONFIDENTIALITY:

- Do not discuss our customers in public areas (i.e., elevators, hallways, cafeteria, etc.)
- Interview customers in privacy. Close doors if available; close curtains when indicated or keep a distance between customers when interviewing them, depending on what's feasible.
- Communicate with our customers' families and significant others in a private manner.
- Respect our co-workers' privacy by eliminating gossip. Our customers also hear this unprofessional talk.
- Telephone conversations between employees and customers should always be conducted with discretion.
- Patient records must be kept confidential.

MODESTY:

- Always knock before entering
- Provide the proper size gowns for our customers.
- Provide sheets or blankets when a patient is being transported.
- Close curtains or doors during examinations, procedures or when otherwise needed.

STRIVE TO MASTER SKILLS:

Employees of Havasu Regional Medical Center will strive to master all the core skills related to their area of job responsibility.

- The best way to teach a skill is to break down the total performance into steps, which the student reassembles.
- The best way to learn a skill is to practice.
- Cross training to other areas is a great way to master new skills and allow for professional growth and will assist in adapting to the ever-changing healthcare environment.
- Consult the monthly education calendar or your supervisor for upcoming opportunities to practice or learn new skills.

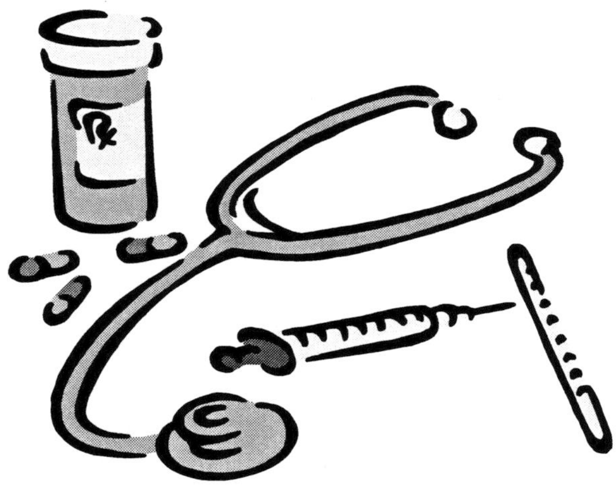

IMAGE:

Our appearance represents our whole organization. Therefore, our grooming and dress will reflect our respect for our customers. While we are on duty, we will first consider our customers' expectations in how we present ourselves. Our manner and expression will convey our concern for and willingness to serve our customers. We will take pride in our facility and do our part to maintain an uncluttered and litter-free work place.

Personal appearance:

- Our dress always will be professional, tasteful, tidy and discreet.
- All customers will be greeted with a warm and friendly smile.
- Identification badges will be properly worn.
- Dress code policies will be followed (proper uniform and clothing, jewelry, perfume).
- Good personal hygiene is expected.

Facility and environmental appearance:

- When we come across litter, we will pick it up and dispose of it properly.
- When we spot spills, we will see to it that they are cleaned up. We will be especially concerned about any debris or spill that could cause someone to slip and fall.
- Equipment will be returned to its proper place.

COMMUNICATION:

The goal of communication is understanding. We must be committed to listening attentively to our customers in order to fully understand their needs, including recognition and acceptance of diverse backgrounds. Close attention should be given to both verbal and non-verbal messages. Our messages to our customers should be delivered with courtesy, clarity and care. We must avoid confusing customers and speak in terms they can easily understand.

Greetings and introductions:

- Every customer will be greeted with a warm and friendly smile.
- Employees will introduce themselves.
- Listen to your customers' concerns in ways that show them you care.

Telephone etiquette:

- All employees must know how to operate telephones in their areas. When transferring a call, first provide the caller with the correct number in case the call is lost.
- Calls must be answered within three rings.
- Answer calls by identifying your department and yourself, asking, "How may I help you?" or the equivalent. Speak clearly.
- Get the caller's permission before putting him or her on hold. Thank the caller for holding when you return to that line.
- Return calls promptly

Giving Directions:

- Observe customers and visitors; if someone appears to need directions, offer to help. Let customers know that you will assist them to their destinations. If you are unable to personally escort a customer, take him or her to someone who can.

Customer information and education:

- Collaborate with each patient's physician to help reinforce information that physician has provided.
- Use easily understood and appropriate language when giving patients information about health, special diets, tests, procedures, medications, etc. Avoid technical or professional jargon.
- Reinforce verbal instruction with teaching sheets or other written material whenever possible.
- Customers with special needs (i.e., translation/interpreters for non-English speaking customers, devices for the hearing impaired) will have those needs addressed by appropriate departments.

Confidentiality:

- Information about patients is strictly confidential. Each employee is responsible for ensuring that it is not compromised.
- Information about patients and their care must never be discussed in public areas such as elevators, lobbies, the cafeteria or waiting rooms. Likewise, hospital business should not be discussed in public areas.
- Only house supervisors or community relations staff or administration are allowed to release information about patients. That information is generally limited to the patient's name, age and condition.

Follow-through:

- All employees will provide appropriate information to their supervisors to ensure proper decisions are made based on the hospital's values.

TEAMWORK:

As Havasu Regional Medical Center employees, we are linked to one another by a common purpose: serving our patients and our community. Our co-workers therefore are our teammates. They deserve our respect. Without their contributions, none of us could perform our jobs. Just as we rely on our fellow employees, they rely on us. Each of us has an obligation to our co-workers. Our mission and values will be our guide in the following:

- Rudeness is never appropriate. We must at all times treat one another with courtesy and respect.
- Treat every co-worker as a professional. Recognize that we each have our area of expertise.
- Show consideration. Be sensitive to a fellow employee's inconvenience. Avoid eleventh hour requests. Consider another's priorities in addition to your own.
- Practice good attendance. Excessive absences can create a burden for other team members.
- Be tolerant of fellow employees. Recognize that conflicts may exist among co-workers, but professional courtesy is expected. Set aside differences when working together. Realize we all have personal shortcomings.
- Be supportive of fellow employees. Offer help when possible. Cooperation is expected in the workplace.
- Be loyal to your co-workers and Havasu Regional Medical Center. Do not undermine other people's work. Be discreet about what you say.
- Welcome new employees. Be supportive offering to help and setting an example of cooperation expected in the workplace.
- Be honest in all interactions with co-workers.

- Respect the privacy of fellow employees.
- Do not chastise or embarrass fellow employees in the presence of others.
- Address problems by going to the appropriate supervisor. Remember that non-supervisory employees may not have the authority to make procedural changes.

APPENDIX F

DESCRIPTION OF THE FIVE TYPES OF ROUNDING

This document describes five different types of rounding:

1. Senior leader rounds
2. Manager rounds in your own area
3. Manager rounds in the areas your department serves
4. Nurse leader rounds
5. Service quality rounds

1. Senior leader rounding

Senior leader rounding is primarily focused on visibility and communication with employees.

Who

Chief executive officer, chief operating office, chief medical officer, chief nursing officer, chief financial officer, chief information officer, senior vice presidents, vice presidents, directors.

Purpose

- To be visible
- To model desired behavior
- To get to know staff and learn what's happening in the hospital
- To demonstrate to staff that you support their efforts and that their feedback will be used to make the organization better
- To capture "wins" for middle managers by rewarding and recognizing staff
- To reward and recognize staff's performance or discover areas for improvement
- To engage staff and find out what they need
- To improve communication—you hear from employees and they hear from you
- To show employees that they are valued
- To build trust between staff and management

- To build relationships
- To increase management's understanding of issues facing patients/family members and employees

Preparation

- Start with a good attitude, and know your purpose.
- Do your homework—take time to educate yourself about the unit/department and the staff.
- Take time to clearly identify your expectations of other leaders.
- Share the goals with all leaders, and outline their responsibilities.
- Find out the best time to visit the unit.
- Have a plan for where to go and when.
- Be prepared with a theme—something to say—before you begin.
- Realize that staff and managers will feel uncomfortable at first. No one is sure what to say, so everyone feels awkward.
- Consider arranging with the manager to escort you and introduce you to staff the first few times you go for a visit.
- Ask managers to share names of their staff so you can be familiar with their names and roles.
- Personalize the visit—mention to the staff that the manager mentioned their progress, achievement, and special work.
- Don't only visit areas where you are comfortable. Visit all areas of the hospital over time, not just the high-profile departments or areas for which you are directly responsible.
- Prepare a closing statement.

When to round

Senior leaders should set a schedule to round at times when they will have the most opportunity to interact with staff. Organizations that use several types of rounding may need to round less frequently than organizations that only use one type.

Frequency

Every organization is going to have to determine what schedule works best for them. We recommend that all senior leaders round once a week and that all departments receive rounds at least once every two weeks.

Getting started: Helpful hints

- Remember to ask the name of each person you speak with in each area you are visiting—and remember it! Knowing names makes it easier the next time you visit.
- Try choosing a theme for the day, and ask similar questions or share the same information with everyone you visit that day.
- Try beginning the conversation by talking about something you've observed, and ask the staff member a question about it.
- Pay attention to the tone of your voice as well as the words you choose. Remember, this isn't a quiz; there is no right or wrong answer.
- Mix it up a bit; use rounding as a way to share information you want staff to hear. This can be very effective if all senior team members are giving the same information when they make their rounds during the same week.
- If there's a current event that is of interest to employees, ask them whether they have questions about it.
- If you've seen a staff member provide very good service, begin the conversation by recognizing that work.

What to say

When an organization initiates rounding into its culture, leaders/mangers/employees may need assistance when it comes to the words or questions necessary to effectively communicate with staff and patients. There will be uneasiness at first about why there's an administrator on the unit or in the department. The first order of business is to remove the barrier of anxiety. Drafting an introduction, questions to ask, and a closing statement will ease your anxiety and the employee's.

Introductions

Hello, my name is ______________________, and I am the (title) here at the hospital. I'm making the rounds today.

Sample questions

- Do you have what you need to do your job today?
- I've noticed that the census is high today. What impact is this having on the way you get your work done on the staff here on the unit?
- [In the business office.] I've notice that it's very noisy in here because of the construction going on. What else can be done to make this more tolerable?
- [In the laundry] "It's quite hot in here. How do you keep your energy level up in the heat?"

Closing statement

Thank you [name of staff member you are talking to] for your time and your insights.

Tools for rounding

- Rounding log
- Pad of paper and a pen or pencil
- Business cards
- Instant recognition awards
- Service-recovery tools
- Patient-satisfaction survey
- Employee-satisfaction survey
- Patient list

Hardwiring rounding for senior leaders

- Senior leader rounding training
- Establish a schedule
- Create rounding regions
- Define questions—establish rounding questions
- Create a rounding log
- Follow up on rounding issues
- Discuss rounding results at executive/management and staff weekly meetings as a standing agenda item

Things to be aware of

- Trying to fix a problem that should be handled by the immediate supervisor.
- Being afraid to admit that you don't know the answer to a question. It's Okay to say, "I'm not certain. I'll check on that and get back to you." The responsibility then becomes yours to follow through and follow up with employees.
- Getting involved in long conversations with physicians or other administrators in a work area.
- Getting discouraged. Remember, it's important to employees to see and talk to their leaders.

Evaluate your success

After four to six weeks, assess the following

- How comfortable do you feel with rounding?

- Are you learning useful information from staff?
- Do you enjoy the interactions?
- Have you kept to your planned schedule?
- How do frontline staff feel about this effort?
- Do staff feel better informed about hospital initiatives and news you have discussed with them?
- Do staff report increased visibility of their leaders?
- Do the individuals with whom you interact react positively to your presence?

2. Manager rounding in your own area

Manager rounding in your own area focuses on opening up channels of communication with your own employees.

Purpose

- Fix and monitor systems
- Remove barriers
- Ensure that goals were accomplished
- Model desired behavior
- Coach and counsel
- Talk to employees, and update information
- Reward and recognize staff

Preparation

- Start with a good attitude and know your purpose.
- Check to find out the best time to visit the unit.
- Have a plan for where to go and when.
- Be prepared with a theme—something to say—before you begin.
- Realize that staff may feel uncomfortable at first. No one is sure what to say, so everyone feels awkward.
- Personalize the visit—mention to staff that you recognize their progress, achievement, and special work.
- Prepare a closing statement.

When to round

We recommend that managers set a schedule, paying attention to workload, to round at times when they will have the most opportunity to interact with staff. We acknowledge that sometimes it's more appropriate to round during slow times, because this will give an opportunity for more in-depth discussions. However, rounding during busy times can also send an important message, especially if you pitch in.

Don't forget to round during weekends and off shifts as well.

Frequency

Every organization must determine what schedule works best for them. We recommend that all managers round in their department once a week.

Getting started: Helpful hints

- One approach is to try finding out a little more about employees' personal lives, professional lives, cool projects, or committee work.
- Pay attention to the tone of your voice as well as to the words you choose. Remember, this isn't a quiz—there is no right or wrong answer.
- Mix it up a bit: Use rounding as a way to share information you want staff to hear. This can be very effective if all management team members give the same information when they make their rounds during the same week.
- If there's a current event that is of interest to employees, ask them whether they have questions about it.
- Celebrate, reward, and recognize staff for their progress on a special project.

What to say

Because you are the manager or direct supervisor, there may be a little anxiety but not necessarily. Our best recommendation is to be yourself.

Introductions

Hello, [name of staff member], I'm making the rounds today.

Sample questions

- Do you have what you need to do your job today?
- How is that project you are working on?
- How are the new ______ [equipment or supplies] working?
- What ideas do you have for reducing the noise level in our area?
- How is the service-recovery program working?

Closing statement

Thank you, [name of staff member you are talking to], for your time and your insights.

Tools

- Rounding log
- Pad of paper and a pen or pencil
- Instant recognition awards
- Patient satisfaction survey
- Employee satisfaction survey
- Patient list

Hardwiring rounding in you own area

- Manager rounding training
- Establish a schedule
- Define questions—establish rounding goals
- Create a rounding log
- Follow up on rounding issues
- Discuss rounding results at management and staff weekly meetings as a standing agenda item

Things of which to be aware

- Don't be afraid to admit that you don't know the answer to a question. It's okay to say, "I'm not certain. I'll check on that and get back to you." The responsibility then becomes yours to follow through and follow up with employees.
- Getting discouraged. Remember how important it is to employees to see and talk to their leaders.

Evaluate your success

After four to six weeks, assess the following

- How comfortable do you feel with rounding?
- What are you learning that helps make the department run better?
- How often do you reward and recognize staff?
- What have you done to help improve the work environment?
- Do you enjoy the interactions?
- Have you kept to your planned schedule?
- How do frontline staff feel about this effort?

- Do staff feel better informed about hospital initiatives and news you have discussed with them?
- Do the individuals with whom you interact react positively to your presence?

3. Manager rounding in areas your department serves

Manager rounding in areas your department serves focuses on opening up channels of communication with your internal customers

Purpose

- Achieve operational excellence
- Seek ways to enhance and improve service
- Understand the customers' point of view and what their needs are
- Build relationships and reduce barriers
- Enhance communication
- Meet with leaders to share with them that they are very important customers
- Review what has been accomplished and what still needs attention
- Provide timelines for issues to be resolved and work to get done
- Follow-up to ensure that gains are sustained

Preparation

- Start with a good attitude and know your purpose.
- Do your homework—take time to educate yourself about the unit/department and staff.
- Check to find out the best time to visit the unit/department.
- Have a plan for where to go and when.
- Be prepared with something to say before you begin.
- Realize that staff and managers may feel uncomfortable at first. No one is sure what to say, so everyone feels awkward.
- Consider arranging with the manager to escort you, introducing you to staff the first few times you go for a visit.
- Personalize the visit—mention to the staff that the manager mentioned their progress, achievement, and special work.
- Prepare a closing statement.

When to round

Work out your schedule with the leader—your colleague—in the other unit/department. This type of rounding should always be done with the other department's needs in mind. Keep in mind that manager rounding in areas your department serves could take on the form of an open forum versus a traditional walk around.

Don't forget to round during weekends and off shifts as well.

Frequency

Conduct rounds weekly with a goal of visiting each service department at least once a month.

Getting started: Helpful hints

Try beginning the conversation by talking about something you've observed, and ask staff a question about it:

- Pay attention to the tone of your voice as well as to the words you choose. Remember, this isn't a quiz; there is no right or wrong answer.
- If you're aware of a staff member who sets a great example of how your departments can work well together, begin the conversation by recognizing that fact.

What to say

When an organization initiates rounding in areas you serve, employees will have questions like "What is this?" "Why are we doing this?" "What's the benefit?" To ease the awkwardness and answer employee questions we recommend planning your introduction, questions, and closing statement.

Introductions

Hello, [name of staff member], I'm making the rounds in your area today.

Sample questions

- What's one thing we should do every day?
- What's one thing we should never do again?
- Is our department responsive to your needs?
- How well do we communicate what services we offer?
- Has someone in our group been especially helpful?
- When you have a problem, do you know how to call? Are they courteous?
- What could our group do more of? Less of?

- What is the best service we provide? Why?
- When you are frustrated with us, what has usually happened? How can we prevent it?

Closing statement

Thank you [name of staff member you are talking to] for your time and your insights.

Tools

- Note pad and pen or pencil
- Rounding log
- Business cards
- Instant recognition awards
- Patient satisfaction survey
- Employee satisfaction survey
- Patient list

Hardwiring interdepartmental rounding

- Manager rounding training
- Establish a schedule
- Create rounding regions
- Define questions—establish rounding questions
- Create a rounding log
- Follow up on rounding issues
- Discuss rounding results at management and staff weekly meetings as a standing agenda item

Things of which to be aware

- Getting involved in long conversations with physicians or other administrators in a work area.
- Being afraid to admit that you don't know the answer to a question. It's okay to say, "I'm not certain. I'll check on that and get back to you." The responsibility then becomes yours to follow through and follow up with employees.
- Getting discouraged. Remember how important it is to employees to see and talk to their leaders.

Evaluate your success

After four to six weeks, assess the following:

- How comfortable do you feel with rounding?
- Are you learning things that help our departments work better together?
- Are you learning useful information from the staff?
- What are some of the ways your departments are working together better?
- Do you enjoy the interactions?
- Have you kept to your planned schedule?
- How do frontline staff feel about this effort?
- Do the individuals you interact with react positively to the interaction?

4. Nurse leader rounding

Nurse leader rounding focuses on the patient and families who are in the nursing unit. The secondary benefit to this type of rounding is increased visibility and communication with employees.

Purpose

- Fix systems
- Be visible to patients and families
- Model behavior
- Get to know patients and staff and learn what's happening in the organization
- Identify, decrease, and remove barriers
- Reward and recognize staff or discover areas for improvement
- Set expectations with patients and family members
- Build rapport with patients and staff

Preparation

Start with a good attitude and know your purpose.

- Determine the best time to visit patients on the unit.
- Have a plan for where to go and when.
- Be prepared with something to say before you begin.
- Realize that staff and patients may feel uncomfortable at first. No one is sure what to say, so everyone feels awkward.
- Prepare a closing statement.

When to round

Nurse leaders should set their schedule to round at times when they have the best opportunity to interact with patients. Our recommendation would be first thing in the morning and when family members are present. In this way, you can observe the previous night shift's work, check the status of patient rooms, IV fluids, bedside commodes, etc.

Don't forget to round occasionally during weekends and off shifts as well.

Frequency

Each organization will have to determine what schedule is best for them. We recommend at a minimum nurse leaders round with a goal of rounding with each admitted patient at least once during their stay. Typically, nurse leaders round for two to four hours every day.

What to say

Preparation is the key to successful and efficient nurse leader rounding. We recommend preparing an opening statement, a list of questions or theme for the rounds, and a closing statement.

Introductions

Hello, [patient name], I am [your name/title] on this unit and I'm doing the rounds this morning. We want to assure you that we will do everything possible to take excellent care of you. But we can't do this alone, we need your help. How was your night?

Sample questions to ask patients and family

Ask the patient these specific questions about how staff care for them. Note that patients who are very ill may not be good candidates for rounding, but their family members are good candidates for rounding.

- What responses are you looking for when you share your concerns and complaints?
- How can staff include you in decisions and treatments? What went well, what could we have done better?
- What does staff sensitivity to inconvenience mean to you? How could we improve?
- What do you need for emotional/spiritual support while you're in the hospitalized?
- What do you expect us to do to show concern for your privacy?
- How can we help decrease the noise level? What noises are interfering with your rest?

Closing statement

Thank you [name of patient or family member you are talking to] for your time and your insights.

Things of which to be aware

- Getting involved in long conversations with physicians or other administrators in a work area.
- Being afraid to admit that you don't know the answer to a question.
- Getting discouraged. Remember how important it is to employees to see and talk to their leaders.

Tools for rounding

- Rounding log
- Pad of paper and a pen or pencil
- Business cards
- Instant recognition awards
- Service recovery tools
- Patient satisfaction survey
- Employee satisfaction survey
- Patient list

Hardwiring nurse leader rounding

- Nurse leader rounding training
- Establish a schedule
- Define questions—establish rounding questions
- Create a rounding log
- Follow up on rounding issues
- Discuss rounding results at management and staff weekly meetings as a standing agenda item

Evaluate your success

After four to six weeks, assess the following:

- How comfortable you feel with rounding?
- Are you learning useful information from patients and their families?
- What problems or inefficiencies have you identified or fixed?
- How often do you reward and recognize staff?
- Do you enjoy the interactions?
- Have you kept to your planned schedule?
- How does frontline staff feel about this effort?
- Do the individuals you interact with react positively?

5. Service quality rounding

Focused on patients and families within the facility, not necessarily in your unit.

Who
Service quality rounding can be conducted by a wide range of individuals, from the CEO to a quality improvement staff member to a frontline nurse.

Purpose

- Fix systems
- Be visible
- Model behavior
- Get to know patients and staff and learn what's happening in the organization
- Identify, decrease, and remove barriers
- Reward and recognize staff or discover areas for improvement
- Set expectations with patients and family members
- Build rapport with patients and staff

Preparation

- Start with a good attitude and know your purpose.
- Do your homework—know the unit and the staff.
- Check to find out the best time to visit the unit.
- Have a plan for where to go and when.
- Be prepared with a theme—something to say—before you begin.
- Realize that staff and patients may feel uncomfortable at first. No one is sure what to say, so everyone feels awkward.
- Prepare a closing statement.

When to round
Service quality rounds should be scheduled when staff would have the best opportunity to interact with patients and family members. This can be at any time of the day. Sometimes when the organization is the busiest is the best time to find things to improve upon.

Don't forget to round occasionally during weekends and off shifts as well.

Frequency

Each organization will have to determine what schedule is best for them. We recommend at a minimum that service quality rounds occur on a daily basis, with a minimum goal of rounding with each admitted patient at least once during their hospitalization.

What to say

When an organization initiates service quality rounding into its culture, leaders/mangers/staff may need assistance when it comes to the words or questions necessary to communicate effectively with staff and patients. We recommend preparing an opening statement, list of questions or theme for the rounds, and a closing statement.

Introductions

Hello, my name is ________________I'm the [your title] of the hospital. I wanted to say hello and make sure that your needs are being met. We're sorry you're sick, but we would like to thank you for allowing us the opportunity to take care of you and your healthcare needs. If there is anything that I can help you with, here is my card. Please don't hesitate to let me know.

Sample questions

These questions tend to be general open-ended questions:

- For anyone but the CEO: My boss won't let me come back to my office until I have 100 ideas on how to improve the hospital. Can you give me one or two ideas?
- Do you have a sense of your care plan?
- Do you have a sense of when you will be discharged?

Note that patients who are very ill may not be good candidates for rounding, but their family members are good candidates for rounding

Closing statement

Thank you [name of patient or family member you are talking to] for your time and your insights.

Tools

- Rounding log
- Business cards
- Pad of paper and a pen or pencil

- Instant recognition awards
- Service-recovery tools
- Patient satisfaction survey
- Employee satisfaction survey
- Patient list

Hardwiring service quality rounding

- Service quality rounding training
- Establish a schedule
- Create rounding regions
- Define questions—establish rounding questions
- Create a rounding log
- Follow up on rounding issues
- Discuss rounding results at executive/management and staff weekly meetings as a standing agenda item

Things of which to be aware

- Getting involved in long conversations with physicians or other administrators in a work area.
- Being afraid to admit that you don't know the answer to a question.
- Getting discouraged. Remember how important it is to employees to see and talk to their leaders.

Evaluate your success

After four to six weeks, assess the following:

- How comfortable do you feel with rounding?
- Are you learning useful information from patients and family members?
- What improvements have been implemented?
- Do you enjoy the interactions?
- Have you kept to your planned schedule?
- How do frontline staff feel about this effort?
- Do the individuals you interact with react positively to your presence?

APPENDIX G

TOOLS FOR ROUNDING

This appendix contains five rounding log forms that can be used by senior leaders, managers (rounding in their own area or in areas their departments serve), nurse leaders, and service quality personnel.

In general, these forms provide a list of questions to ask or information to share during the visit, examples of "words that work" to initiate and transition and end conversation, and an area to indicate names of staff and reasons why the individual rounding recognized them for service excellence.

SENIOR LEADER ROUNDING LOG

DATE:____________________ TIME: ______________________________
UNIT/DEPARTMENT:____
NAME:__________________________ TITLE: ______________________________

WORDS THAT WORK
"Hello, my name is_________. I am the _______ (your title) at the hospital. I'm making the rounds today."

QUESTIONS TO ASK AND INFORMATION TO SHARE

Do you have what you need to do your job?

____
____
____

I've noticed that the census is high today. What impact is this having on the way you get your work done on the staff here on the unit?

____
____
____

NOTES:

REWARD AND RECOGNITION

NAME: ____

REASON: ____

NAME: ____

REASON: ____

______________ **Discussed rounding with staff prior to today's rounds**
Initials/Date

______________ **Discussed rounding with staff after today's rounds**
Initials/Date

MANAGER ROUNDING (IN YOUR OWN AREA) LOG

DATE:______________________________ TIME: ______________________________

UNIT/DEPARTMENT:____

NAME:______________________________ TITLE: ______________________________

WORDS THAT WORK

"Hello, ____________________ (name of staff member), I'm making the rounds today."

QUESTIONS TO ASK AND INFORMATION TO SHARE

How is the new equipment working?

____

____

____

What ideas do you have to reduce the noise level in our work area?

____

____

____

NOTES:

REWARD AND RECOGNITION

NAME: ____

REASON: ____

NAME: ____

REASON: ____

_______________ **Discussed rounding with staff prior to today's rounds**

Initials/Date

_______________ **Discussed rounding with staff after today's rounds**

Initials/Date

MANAGER ROUNDING (IN AREAS YOUR DEPARTMENT SERVES) LOG

DATE:____________________ TIME: ____________________
UNIT/DEPARTMENT:____________________
NAME:____________________ TITLE: ____________________

WORDS THAT WORK

"Hello, __________________ (name of staff member), I'm making the rounds today."

QUESTIONS TO ASK AND INFORMATION TO SHARE

What's one thing we should do every day?

____

What's one thing we should never do again?

____

Is our department responsive to your needs?

____

REWARD AND RECOGNITION

NAME: ____

REASON: ____

NAME: ____

REASON: ____

______________ **Discussed rounding with staff prior to today's rounds**
Initials/Date

______________ **Discussed rounding with staff after today's rounds**
Initials/Date

NOTES:

NURSE LEADER ROUNDING LOG

DATE:________________________________ TIME: ________________________
UNIT/DEPARTMENT:____
NAME:________________________ TITLE: ____________________________
ROOM: ________________________

TOP PATIENT SATISFACTION PRIORITIES

1.
2.

WORDS THAT WORK

"Hello, [patient name], I am __________ [your name/title] on this unit and I'm doing the rounds this morning. We want to assure you that we will do everything possible to take excellent care of you. But we can't do this alone; we need your help. How was your night?

QUESTIONS TO ASK

What are three things that we need to know about you that will help us care for you?

____

____

Have you voiced a concern or complaint about the care or services you are receiving during your hospitalization?

____

What kind of response to a concern or complaint would be meaningful to you?

____

____

What could our staff do to improve how we include you and your family in decisions and treatments? What went well, what could we have done better?

____

____

What do you need for emotional/spiritual support while you're hospitalized?

____

____

SERVICE RECOVERY

Was service recovery needed?______________________________

What was immediate service recovery action?______________________________

____________ **Service Recovery tracking form completed**
Initials/Date

____________ **Discussed rounding with staff prior to today's rounds**
Initials/Date

____________ **Discussed rounding with staff prior to today's rounds**
Initials/Date

NOTES:

SERVICE QUALITY ROUNDING LOG

DATE:______________________________ TIME: ________________________

UNIT/DEPARTMENT:____

NAME:________________________ TITLE: ____________________________

ROOM: ________________________

TOP PATIENT SATISFACTION PRIORITIES

1.
2.
3.

WORDS THAT WORK

"Hello, my name is ______________. I'm the [your title] of the hospital. I wanted to say hello and make sure that your needs are being met. We're sorry you're sick, but we would like to thank you for allowinc
you and your healthcare needs. If there is any
is my card. Please don't hesitate to let me kn

QUESTIONS TO A

My boss won't let me come back to my office until I have 1
hospital. Can you give me one or two ideas?

Do you have a sense of your care plan?

Do you have a sense of when you will be discharged?

SERVICE RECOVERY

Was service recovery needed?____________________

What was immediate service recovery action?__________

____________ **Service recovery tracking form**

Initials/Date

____________ **Discussed rounding with staf**

Initials/Date

____________ **Discussed rounding with staf**

Initials/Date

NOTES: